THE JOURNEY FROM ERROR TO HEIR

An autobiography of a life's journey
from abuse to finding a victory of God's
choosing--far bigger and different from
what I thought victory could ever be

EARNIE LEWIS

InspiringVoices

Inspiring Voices books may be ordered through booksellers or by contacting:

Inspiring Voices
1663 Liberty Drive
Bloomington, IN 47403
www.inspiringvoices.com
1 (866) 697-5313

Because of the dynamic nature of the Internet, any web addresses or
links contained in this book may have changed since publication and
may no longer be valid. The views expressed in this work are solely those
of the author and do not necessarily reflect the views of the publisher,
and the publisher hereby disclaims any responsibility for them.

Any people depicted in stock imagery provided by Thinkstock are models,
and such images are being used for illustrative purposes only.
Certain stock imagery © Thinkstock.

ISBN: 978-1-4624-1140-5 (sc)
ISBN: 978-1-4624-1139-9 (e)

Library of Congress Control Number: 2015911970

Print information available on the last page.

Inspiring Voices rev. date: 07/28/2015

CONTENTS

Part III
Finding Freedom

FOREWORD & ACKNOWLEDGEMENTS

Taking on the task of writing an autobiography that is authentic and transparent has been monumental. I've never been one to run from conflict or to procrastinate on a job needing done. However, that hasn't been the case in addressing this book. From the viewpoint of man, I'd be called a genuine procrastinator and an avoider of conflict in this event. However, from a spiritual viewpoint, God didn't have me ready in all the areas of freedom & victory that He wanted me to know before undertaking this.

My human nature has always been to use any experience I've encountered or one someone I know has encountered to grow and mature. However, my childhood sexual abuse and physical/emotional abuse were too graphic, painful and shameful for me to use until my later years in life. I write this because I want any reader to know the purpose of this writing isn't simply to tell my story. However, it is intended to be:

- a testimony of God's amazing healing in today's world;
- a guide to freedom for someone stuck in the secrets of abuse and the damage it creates; and

- a book of HOPE for anyone tackling or wishing to tackle a problem bigger for them than life itself.

The title of my book--<u>The Journey From Error to Heir</u> came from a sermon my pastor gave in the fall of 2014. He didn't use this title, but he did emphasize the fact that we are all heirs of Christ if we accept His work for us on the cross. Even though I'd heard this many times in my life, when I was hearing it this time the first thought that came to me was the fact I'd always thought of myself as an error and this word rhymed with heir. The words are homonyms, sounding the same with different meanings and spelling. Why would God bring a 10th child into a family of 12 children when much of his childhood was filled with sexual abuse from a brother 10 years older than he and to experience the physical and emotional abuse from his dad? The thought I was an error was deeply embedded in the primal beliefs about myself.

A ministry called Celebrate Recovery became the door God opened for me in 2007 to begin my road to freedom. I had heard about this program from a brother-in-law of my wife who led it for his church in Western Oregon. A one day seminar introducing it came to Boise, Idaho in June of 2007. My wife and I organized six of us from our church to attend it. I ordered all the leadership materials necessary for getting it started. In preparing myself with the materials, I found I was needing it, and should not be leading it. God took care of the leadership need and I was able to begin this journey early in 2008.

It has been amazing to find what God is pointing out to me just in the writing of this. I truly am a gardener at heart and so the analogy God gave me this morning allowed me to understand something that was starting to haunt me in the writing of the book. In order to bare my soul in this book, I have to reveal the part of my life that I've kept a secret. Even though I've walked the path of recovery for it and told it to many groups, I've never come close to placing it into the "hands of the world". So, now that I'm actually putting my life into full transparency I find myself awaking in the night with much of the same fears I've had throughout my life. In journaling about this during my devotions this morning I asked God what it meant. He allowed me to compare this to my gardening. He reminded me how my body responds each spring to all the shoveling, pruning, rototilling I do to prepare for the coming year. I immediately knew he was talking about my sore muscles and stiff back which happens in the first week or two of spring work. He said that the fears and concerns I encounter are no different. They are just what the human mind and heart do when you stretch them. These are emotional responses to strenuous work. I don't stop gardening because of the sore muscles. If I did the crop would never be harvested. The response is the same for the book. If I stop the writing because of fears and anxiety the crop can never be harvested. So folks, the book is going to be written. I'm on assignment.

There is a yearning inside me to ensure the voice of God's Spirit is continuously present throughout the book. I have read and reread this manuscript to take out the "Earnie's" in it. Earnie didn't find himself solely in this journey. What he found is a Magnificent, tender-loving God who has never abandoned nor forsaken him. This God of mine and ours is ever seeking to finish the creation He started when we were first conceived. Man interferes in this process but He never abandons. He waits patiently for us. He has been the motivator for this manuscript and the author I want to be sure is named. I am forever grateful for Jesus Christ, my Risen Savior, Redeemer and Lord.

I will never be able to adequately thank the host of people who have been integral in this journey from exposing the abuse to finding freedom from it. My wife Kathy stands at the top of the list. Little did I know what a gift God was giving me when she said yes to marrying me. She is the first person I ever told about my past thinking no one would ever want me close to them if they knew the truth about me. Her responses were always and continue to be ones of support, comfort and encouragement. Right under her name is the name of a very close friend who never wavered from his relentless support and Godly guidance. His name is Mike and he is not just a best friend, but he is also a 40+ year singing buddy. Next are two counselors who were God's instruments in pointing out many of the steps to freedom the book clarifies. Family members, two of which I want to name, Alice and Bonnie (sisters) need to be recognized for seeing well beyond the abuse of a brother, to see a brother who was already to them an heir of Jesus, (I tear up just writing this). Many Celebrate Recovery leaders in our group, one for which I need to name, Carol. She endlessly focused me back to who God created and not to the lies I thought man had created. Lastly, the ones who took their time to thoughtfully and meticulously read this manuscript for editing purposes. My fears often screamed that I was being too descriptive or graphic. Their guidance allowed me to be better assured that the book is ready for an audience of readers. Kathy Tolan, you have been a long-time friend of my family and me. Thank you for using your expertise to give this help. I've known most of my life that if I ever wrote this book, you would be the first person from which I want guidance. Your kind words and clarifying help mean the world to me. Nancy Chopko, I've not known you too many years, but I've loved the few I've had working with you. I've enjoyed your ability to identify a problem and reroute it to success. I learned that you were an avid reader and because you aren't afraid to say the truth, I wanted you to read this book and tell me your objective truth. Thank you for this. My final thanks goes to my daughter Amber. She created the book cover for me. Each of my three daughters have been most encouraging to me in moving forward with this work. When I asked Amber to consider creating the book cover, she did it from the picture God gave her once she'd read the document. Thank you Amber.

PART I

Years of Abuse

CHAPTER 1

Dad

The year was 1950 and the day was July 1st. The location was a farm a couple miles outside a rural town in Southwestern Idaho named Homedale which bordered the Snake River. Harold was packing his fishing gear and corralling some of his boys that early morning. Everett, 21 and Rich, 10 wouldn't be going but Ralph, 18; Herb, 14 and Don, 12 were excited for a day of trout fishing 50 miles into the mountains at Sage Hen Reservoir. If Harold and Opal had talked at all about Opal's pregnancy which was 3 days from the expected arrival, no one knows. Alice was home and almost 16 along with the fact Eunice, 22 and married, just lived a couple miles up the road and had a car. Bonnie was also home but only two years old.

It was early afternoon when Opal announced to Alice she needed to go to the doctor's office in Homedale so he could take her on to the hospital in Caldwell. Alice jumped into gear having Everett run with her to the neighbors. They came and drove Opal and Alice to the doctor. Alice then called Eunice to come. Eunice's husband was a policeman and so he took

Eunice to town in his police car with the siren blowing all the way. Dr. Wolfe announced that this baby was going to be born in the office. There would not be time to get Opal to Caldwell. He quickly prepped Eunice for assisting him. Alice stayed outside with the neighbors. Soon an 8 lb. baby boy was delivered. Eunice and Alice both argue over who swatted his bottom first. None of this mattered to Opal, her only question was, "How much does he weigh?"

Given the fact this new boy was baby number 10, there seemed to be no more names from Harold and Opal. Thus, the children who had lost a cousin in World War II named Ernest Nichols, wanted this boy to be named Ernie. The birth certificate reads Ernest Leon Lewis. However mom always wrote the spelling as Earnest Leon Lewis. So present records all show the spelling of Earnest with an "a".

You might notice I was baby number 10. However, if you count the names of the children mentioned there are a total of nine including me. Dad and Mom's second boy was named Howard, born in 1931. He died very young. I know little about him except he was said to be a "blue baby". It is told he had a heart condition from birth for which doctors didn't have a treatment or cure.

I like to believe that mom and dad were so glad to have me for their newest son that they quickly decided to have another. Ron was born only 10 months and 6 days after me, May 6, 1951. I like to tell him he was a disappointment because our folks' last child came 2 1/2 years after Ron. This was Polly who was finally mom's last caboose. We were actually told that each of the last four were to be the last, but....

Six month after Ron was born in 1951 dad decided he was going to sell the farm and move to Escondido, California.

This wasn't a new idea for him. He and mom had married in California in 1927 moving several times in their early years to different locations between Central and Southern California. It was in 1942 they moved to Idaho for the first time so dad could buy his first farm. Mom's parents, Emmanuel & Susie Wretling had already made this move and dad wanted to make his purchase. In order to do so, he kept all the kids out of school in the fall of '42 so they could pick hops in the Wilder, Idaho area. With the oldest ones joining mom and dad they were able to earn over a $1,000.00 to get the down payment for the farm. The farm house was very small with only two bedrooms, a bath, small kitchen and living room. With so many children, dad added a lean-to where all the boys slept. Now, 9 years later, grandma and grandpa Wretling had already sold their farm and returned to Escondido. Dad had the itch to do the same. In December of '51 he loaded all the children except Eunice who was married and had two children of her own and moved to Escondido joining several relatives living in this area.

The move to Escondido didn't put us right in town. Dad purchased a 10 acre orange grove that had a two bedroom house, one bath, kitchen and living room outside the city limits. It already had a screened porch and so the boys primarily slept in it. I was a year and a half at this time.

My earliest memories of this place and time are very mixed. We lived in this location until May, 1959, a total of almost eight years. It was here that I began to build memories of my father's verbal and physical abuse. Keep in mind I was certainly not the only victim of dad's abuse. Each of the boys received their "fair share". Dad may have had a favorite, but if so, no one felt as though they were it.

5

My younger brother, Ron, and I began to be pitted against one another at times. Dad, and sometimes his brother, would set up wrestling matches or fighting matches. I would cry at these times begging to not have to be involved in this. I didn't want to hurt someone and I hated the thought that I was being required to do so. There was no sport in this for me as there seemed to be for them. This would lead to all kinds of names being given to me with the least of them being ones like "baby" or "little girl." At other times dad and our uncle would take all our clothes off with the exception of our underwear throwing the clothes on the roof of the house. We would be left to find a way to get them down while we ran around feeling fully exposed to everyone. We'd eventually find a way to climb to the roof, get our pants and shirts and redress. All this would be a time of laughter for the adult males. This left me feeling like I was a toy for dad and my uncle. I could be good entertainment for them but in reality I wasn't even that due to the resistance I gave.

The differences in dad's makeup and mine drove me to be with mom and my sisters, primarily Bonnie who was just a couple years older. Over time she and I formed a bond which is deeply embedded in the two of us today. Mom would let me work with her in the yard, garden, kitchen or laundry. Even as a young boy six or seven years old I was allowed to iron dad's hankies. I would even get to sprinkle the laundered clothes needing ironed. It was fun to dip my hand in the bowl of water and flip the moisture onto the clothes dampening them and then rolling them into a tight ball until ironing time. I don't recall mom complimenting me for the tasks I did. Mom had a peacefulness about her so different than dad's nature. I never longed for anything from her except her time. Just being able to do the tasks for her without insult and belittlement was compliment enough.

It was during these early years I began to realize how moody our dad was. He worked an 8:00 am to 5:00 pm job so I quickly learned to be absent when he was around if the moodiness was present. When dad was feeling good he was fun. However, his good moods would then trigger us kids to likewise be less guarded about our behavior. It was then that one of us would say or do something that triggered his anger. This would likely lead to severe spanking (beatings) for everyone around--particularly the boys. These beatings were the kind that kept us out of school due to the bruises and welts. Dad wasn't particular about what he used to beat us. His belt, a limb, a razor strap were most often used, but even when he used his hands, they seemed just as powerful.

One vivid memory for me when I was around five or six was when my younger brother and I had the giggles at the breakfast table. Something had triggered our laughter and even though we were told a couple times to stop as dad was ready to say the blessing, we only temporarily stopped. One of us would let out a little burst of laughter setting off the other one all over again. To end this behavior and out of disgust, dad took my left hand, closest to him, stuck it in the hot oatmeal and prayed. He only let go of it after he finally said, "Amen." All I know from this point was I stopped laughing and screamed only inside. I was quickly learning to do my best to withhold the hurt given from his corrective actions. If we cried too soon or too much his words were something like, "You better stop or I'll really give you something to cry about!" Instead of crying, I kept it inside and then ran outside taking the hose attached to a spigot and let cold water run over it for a time. My entire hand was blistered. I have no memory of what was done after this.

During these young years I had severe thumb sucking and bed wetting problems. It wasn't just me who had them, the boys wet the bed and even the girls sucked their thumbs. In order to break us of the thumb sucking, mom sewed socks onto our pajama sleeves so our fingers didn't show. I don't know if this helped but I do know my brother Ron cried because his pajamas didn't have socks. He felt left out! When my front teeth came in around the age of 6 they were what was called "bucked teeth"--protruding outward. My pet name from dad was Bucky Beaver. Bucky was the comic character for Ipana Toothpaste which advertised at that time in the 50's. I was very embarrassed by this. One day dad told me that if I'd push inward on my front teeth they would straighten. For months when no one was looking I would be pushing in on these four teeth. By the time we moved from California to Oregon this name had vanished so maybe it worked.

Mom tried an abundance of cures for the bedwetting. She would swat us, reward us with a nickel, keep charts--all with no avail. One night she came and awoke Ron and me to take us to the bathroom. (I don't recall this one story but I know it first hand from the number of times it has been told over the years). As mom was herding Ron and me to the bathroom I strayed away in my groggy state. She caught me with my dresser drawer pulled open and I was using it as the toilet wetting on my clothes kept within. I'm sure mom wasn't happy about this, but because it was mom and not dad, it actually became a story that brought laughter rather than painful memories.

The whipping I got from another situation when I was seven years old was what I call my worst in California. It was late spring and one of my older brothers, Don, had come home from Los Angeles where he was attending college. Dad was in one of his great moods. He and Don decided to go into town and get ice cream so mom could make everyone ice cream floats. As dad was backing our car out of the garage (shed) he came within inches of backing over the only bicycle all of us kids had. He had only recently purchased it for us and so it was to be cared for correctly. This threw dad into an immediate explosion. He came and found Ron and me thinking one of us had done this. Remember, this is southern California in late spring so it is already hot. We kids never wore shoes at home during these days. Thus, footprints were everywhere around the bike. Dad had Ron and I put our foot in the prints. At that point in our lives I was bigger than Ron so my foot fit closer to the print. He asked if I had left the bike there and I repeatedly said I hadn't been riding it and, "No, I did not leave it there."

Dad instantly thought he knew it was me and asked why I was lying. Out of desperation I finally said, "If I did leave it there I don't remember it." The evening had been destroyed and I was now going to pay for it. He started dragging me to the house yelling for mom. He told her to take me in the bedroom and give me a spanking for leaving the bike behind the car and then lying about it. Mom quickly obeyed and took me in their bedroom. She swatted me a couple times which were more like pats on the bottom. The next thing that happened surprised me because when mom left, my brother Don came in the room. He was next to discipline me. He swatted me several times scolding me for ruining his coming home for the weekend. The worst was yet to come. In walked dad with his face full of rage. He pulled off his belt and the lashings began. On the back, on the buttocks, on the thighs and back of calves, the lashings were delivered. Dad wanted me to confess to lying but I would not cave in to lying about something that wasn't a lie. I guess he must have been spent because he eventually stopped. I have no more memories of this night.

My next memory was that on Monday and Tuesday of the next week I didn't go to school. Ron didn't either. He and I were kept home and allowed to go to work with dad. Dad drove a semi-truck hauling sand and gravel. He would always take a cold lunch in his black, metal lunchbox and would stop along the way to eat whenever noontime came. This particular time, he was in route somewhere into the foothills. I recall a pull-off where dad stopped the truck along with another driver named Jake. He and dad were good friends. I'm sure Jake had to notice the marks I had, but nothing was said. Ron and I were able to carry our own sack lunches and eat with dad and Jake that day. At the age I was, it still seemed like a treat for Ron and me to go with dad in the big truck.

All these years later I've learned that this, in dad's mind, was his way of saying, "sorry," for his actions. Everyone of us kids can recall many incidents when a little something: popsicles, ice cream cone, a trip to town, would follow a beating. Once in a while it was appreciated. However, as each of us got older this behavior of dad was loathed knowing what had happened was so superior to his incidental gifts.

CHAPTER 2

Rich

Growing up in the country has always been a plus for me. I like the benefits and the excitement a town can offer, but my heart has always yearned to be in the country and my hands have always loved being in the dirt. I didn't know this as a young boy, but I certainly know this today.

The 10 acre orange grove we had outside Escondido, California was a rich place for all of dad and mom's kids. The older ones were glad to be close to town and several of them finished their schooling while we lived there. The uglier side of this however was because the ten acres allowed Rich to have a vast amount of private property to hide his behavior. Before delving into this time I need to give some background about him and our family. Two of mom and dad's boys had what I'd call today--learning delays. In the times of my early childhood the two of them were called retarded, stupid, slow and other less palatable names. Everett was the older one with delays. He was actually 21 years older than I and was institutionalized when I was seven years old due to severe emotional outbursts. All of us kids believe these were largely created due to the extensive abuse he had from our dad and his inability to express this in a more socially acceptable way. My only personal memories of Everett were that he liked me. He would say just that. He would carry me on his shoulders in the orange grove as an older adult would do for a little tyke. One time I was on his shoulders when he stepped onto a pile of boards. Under them, unbeknownst to us, was a hornet's nest. They swarmed us with a vengeance. Everett ran as fast as he could but there were no less than eight to ten that stung both of us during the get-away.

My memories of Rich were much more vivid. Rich was ten years older than I with a birthday just 23 days after mine. In fact he shared this birth date with a sister, Alice, who was six years older than he. Rich was quiet and shy. He rarely looked anyone in the eye. We kids knew him well enough as we got older to know he was highly intelligent in the world of electronics. He understood radios and televisions as though he created them. He could take anyone's appliance and quickly analyze and then repair it. Over the years he collected many tubes and transistors for the radios and televisions of the time and would successfully repair them. This gift however, was never to be complimented by dad. To dad Everett and Rich were an embarrassment and a humiliation. He did his best to beat their stupidity out of them or humiliate them into a better behavior. Little did he understand the emotional harm he was instilling in them as he tried to beat or humiliate the other out.

It would have been around 1954 when the first of Rich's sexual endeavors began with me. He would have reached puberty by this time. I don't have a clear date as to when this began, but I do have a clear memory of it happening. Rich enticed me into the orange grove to play. Once we got deep into the orchard he took my clothes off and sat me on a tree limb high enough I wouldn't jump but low enough he could reach me easily. The details need not be disclosed as to the ways he abused me, but he kept me there until he was gratified. I was three or four when all this began. I cannot recall the feelings I had at this time. It would be 35 years later when I first went to counseling that I felt my first feelings. It took another 20 years before finally, in therapy, I not only felt the feelings I had but also began to work through them. Later I will disclose some in-depth therapy that was used to help me give perspective to this abuse. I really don't know how many times this happened in the orchard, but I do know it continued throughout our years in California. I have vague memories of someone else being there with Rich in a couple of these moments. In reality I believe this person was masturbating with Rich but I was there only as Rich's stimulant.

CHAPTER 3

California Years

Our California years weren't all about abuse. During these years I was taken to church most every week. It is funny that I have no memories of dad going, but I know he must have gone some of the time. I recall sitting in church by mom who would have her little cache of things for us kids and me to do so we wouldn't become too fidgety. The one I recall best was taking her hankie and carefully folding it into a triangle. Taking each of the pointed ends and rolling them to the center created two coils of the hankie. I then had to take the individual ends of the hankie and begin to pull them apart. This created what mom said was a cradle and there would be two little tightly coiled parts of the hankie. She told me they were twins and I could rock them back and forth. When I try this with my own grandkids today they quickly set it aside. It is much more fun to get grandpa's iphone and play the apps on it!

At the Free Methodist Church in Escondido I got my first foundation in how to live right. Even at this young age I knew some of the behaviors of my older brothers and sisters were rebellious acts against dad's treatment. They all smoked but one, they all drank and some excessively. A couple of them were repeatedly arrested for ill conduct. By this time my oldest sister had already divorced and married again. She was still in Idaho. One brother in California had married with two children and divorced. Another brother had married and his wife was in prison. Somehow I knew these actions connected to dad and rebellion. I knew I wanted to have a different outcome to my life, but wasn't sure how to make it happen.

Once or twice a year dad would take our family to the ocean. Because we lived only 25 miles from the Mexico border, we would often go into Mexico for these camping excursions. The longer ones would have us there for a week, shorter ones would be for a weekend or an extended weekend. There dad and the older boys fished. Ron and I would find day long opportunities to explore. We'd make friends with the children who lived along the beach. One incident I recall was an inlet where we discovered a sandy beach covered with thousands of sand dollars. I had no idea these were living creatures. I got a bucket and filled it with them. A couple days later when we were driving home dad kept yelling about something stinking so badly. When we got to our home an hour later he found my bucket. That was when I was told these sand dollars had been alive but not anymore. Also, that was the source of the bad smell.

In these days the borders between our United States and Mexico were easy to cross. Often my older brothers would go there in the late afternoon and bring home abalone by the gunnysacks. Clams and other shellfish were abundant too, along with deep sea fish like tuna and sea bass. I learned to love seafood from a very young age.

I have no memory of my youngest sister Polly being born. I was three and a half when she entered our lives. I do recall a crib being in the living room where she slept. She was a girl and a baby so we didn't have too much to do with her at that point in our lives. Polly was a tomboy early on. She loved to climb the pecan tree in our yard. She was around four when she fell out of the tree. In doing so she scraped against a metal post cutting a gash in her leg just below the knee. It was deep and exposed the bone. My brother Ron and a neighbor friend were with her. They carried her by the arms and legs to the house screaming she was dying. Dad wasn't home from work. I don't remember if Alice were already at our house or if we called her to come. She loaded Polly and mom to head to the doctor. In route they passed dad who saw them. Alice turned them over to dad and he took them on to the hospital where they gave Polly many stitches and proclaimed she would live. That was a big relief to us little ones who were home anxiously waiting this news!

When I was old enough, six or seven, I planted the little sandbox we had into a garden of corn. I don't recall where I got the seed, but I had it and thus created my first garden. By the time school was out and dad was going to Mexico for a week my corn was from knee to hip high. I don't recall if that height was my young height or if that were an adult height. It doesn't really matter. My older brother Herb was living in a small trailer on our place at the time. He told me he'd water my corn while we were gone for the week. When I returned the corn wasn't just wilted, it was practically crisp and brown. Southern California in June is HOT and my garden was sand. I'm not sure I ever forgave Herb for this atrocity. I'm sure he had no idea just how important this garden was to his little brother! It is a fun thing to hold over his head today however. In fact, my love for gardening was apparent enough that my siblings named me "Tingus Fauchey." He was a Chinese gardener who had a TV program in the 50's. Today I'm still called Ting or Fauchy at times by the older ones. That was a comforting name unlike Bucky Beaver.

California was a state that offered kindergarten in the 50's. When I was five years old I started and would take my towel each day for the nap time. I would ride a bus to school but someone had to pick me up because I don't think there was busing for the half-day program. My dad owned a Model A Ford at the time and one of my older brothers came and got me from school in it. We were almost home, making the last turn off of Felicita Road when the steering froze. Whoever was driving went head on into a telephone pole. The impact threw me into the dash of the car. It would have been nothing today with seatbelts, but those didn't exist then. I must have been knocked out for a moment because my next memory is a big goose egg on my forehead and being on the couch.

Towards the end of first grade our school put on a musical production for parents. Mom never drove during her life. I remember Aunt Billie coming and getting mom and me and taking us to the school. Uncle Will stayed with dad. When we got home Mom and Aunt Billie asked me to sing one of the more exuberant songs from the program for dad and Uncle Will. I did and they all applauded when I was done. I must have been feeling really good about it too as I remember asking if they wanted me to sing it again. Dad said, "No, once was enough." My feeling good was short lived.

In second grade I was in love with my teacher. I remember she was blonde and wore beautiful red lipstick. I truly misbehaved a great deal that year. I honestly don't know if it was because I sought her attention in any way I could get it, I just know I thought I had found true love. I'm not sure what I did to get sat under her desk routinely, but that was her primary place to put me. There she kept her purse--great find! In it was her red lipstick. I used it to mark all over the under part of her desk with it. She also smoked I found out. I knew that was bad because many of my older brothers and sisters smoked and dad was always telling them that it was bad. So, I broke all her cigarettes in half putting them back in the purse. In all of this she never yelled at me or sent me to the principal. I recall that after the noon recess we were to put our heads on the desk and rest. Who could ever rest after recess was my thinking! I would suck on the tail of my shirt during this time. I likely did this since I couldn't suck my thumb any longer and surely wouldn't do it at school. She would come by my desk and rub her hand up and down my back. Being an educator myself now, I realize just how much she must have understood about this young boy.

I have always been left-handed. It was this 2nd grade teacher who taught me how to turn my paper the opposite direction so I didn't have to cock my wrist in order to write with the paper slanted the way a right-hander does. I was the only left-hander of the twelve kids. In fact, I was the only left-hander with almost white, blonde hair and very blue eyes. Even though a few others in the family had blue eyes, no one had this mix of traits. I was six or seven when I asked mom if I were adopted? I'll never forget her response, "Good grief, why would I want to adopt a child when I already have so many?" She then went on to tell me I was her Swede. Her father, Grandpa Wretling, was born in Sweden. She said I was very much like him. He loved to garden like me and wasn't skilled mechanically and couldn't seem to understand the engineering side of all this also like me. He wasn't left-handed but his youngest son was. That was enough information for this little one to know I had a place in the family. Grandpa & Grandma Wretling were my most favorite relatives so the very thought I was like grandpa bolstered my spirits immensely.

Somehow, the idea I was different from my brothers in numerous ways was always just behind the first thought I had. Ron loved to play sports and throw the ball whether football or baseball. I wasn't good at either. This interest in sports was huge in dad as well as all my brothers except Rich and Everett. Ron liked to pretend we were quarterbacks or baseball pitchers and he'd throw the ball to me naming which quarterback or pitcher he was pretending to be at the moment according to the ball we were throwing. I was to do the same but I could only name Johnny Unitas, a name I knew as someone's quarterback. In baseball I knew the pitchers Don Drysdale and Sandy Koufax who played for the Dodgers. These 3 names were used so much in the house that I could remember them. I still remember them all these years later. It is my claim to sports fame. It seemed Ron could name dozens of them and I wondered why he was so smart and I wasn't.

I loved school. I can't remember ever having a bad day there whether it was in California or later in Oregon. I always looked forward to everyday of school. As I got into third grade I discovered white paste and red pencils. The white paste became everyday's dessert and snack. I loved dipping my finger into the jar and eating as much as I could without getting caught. I don't recall my other teachers using red pencils, but my third grade teacher did--and a lot! I began to take her pencil off her desk whenever she wasn't by it. By the end of that year I had a bread bag full of them. She often asked the class if anyone had seen her red pencil and no one confessed and I remained quiet. It was at the end of this grade dad moved us to Eastern Oregon. I somehow snuck the bag of pencils all the way to the farm without being caught. Somewhere along the line I discarded them. I just couldn't live with the guilt. Later in college I sent a check to the Felicita Elementary School in Escondido, California to pay for all these pencils. If I intended to be a teacher, I couldn't go into the profession with this huge theft hanging over my head.

I'm sure dad and mom did much planning before our move to Oregon. I do recall dad making a trip to find a farm in the early spring. I even recall the conversation that he found one. None of this meant anything to me. I hadn't ever moved as far as memory served so I had nothing tangible to attach these conversations to. The concrete part came when dad and mom came to the school to pick us up. It was in later May, 1959. School wouldn't end until mid-June. Dad had occupancy of the farm on June 1st so he was eager to get us moved. Our place was also sold so we may have needed to vacate our home there. These details were nothing to me at the time. I recall the principal coming out onto the playground saying to take ten minutes to tell everyone good-bye. I remember hugging a few friends and that was it. We spent that night with my Aunt Vee and Uncle John who lived outside Escondido. Dad and mom had the station wagon packed along with a U-haul trailer we were pulling. There would be seven of us making the move. It would be dad, mom, Rich (18), Bonnie (10), myself (8), Ron (8), and Polly (4). The rest of the older brothers and sisters were either married or young adults with jobs keeping them from moving with us.

CHAPTER 4

Oregon

The move to Oregon was an adventure for a boy just weeks from turning nine. School had already ended when we arrived so we were officially into summer vacation. We were told we had cows on the farm. I had seen them before but had never been up to one or touched one. Now we would be milking them day and night--HOW FUN! That attitude changed dramatically within a few weeks!

We were unable to move directly into our farm house. The sellers couldn't move to give us occupancy until June 1st and we arrived about two weeks earlier. We stayed the first week with friends of Mom and Dad named Eddie and Mary Nelson. They had a ranch by Jordan Valley, Oregon where we kids roamed the sage brush hills and I discovered rocks like I'd never seen before along with arrow heads and much more. The following week we came to Eddie and Mary's farm closer to Adrian, Oregon in the area called Ridgeview. Here we met the first of the Nelson families we would soon become very close to because all of them attended the same little Free Methodist Church in Adrian.

The next week we moved onto our farm. The house had a 3/4 basement. It was an unfinished one, but it became the bedroom for Rich, Ron and me. The two bedrooms upstairs were for mom and dad and the other for Bonnie and Polly. Wow, what room we thought we had! The basement had two fairly large rooms and a storage room where mom put her hundreds of jars for canning. The empty jars in the winter months became great containers for the "pee cans" we were to have under our bed. Mom was never too happy to find that we'd used another jar for this purpose instead of the three pound Folgers coffee cans she'd routinely give us. However, she was always mom about her treatment of us.

The days of adventure on the farm quickly turned into days of labor. The cows that were so fun to think about were now the ones needing to be herded morning and night to the barn for milking. They didn't milk themselves, either. We did have electric milkers which made the process easier. Only the stripping was a remembrance of long ago when milking was all done by hand. The milking by hand did happen once in a while when the power would go out.

In the school we attended in Escondido, one day each week a banker would come to the school and collect the coins each child wanted to put in their "account". This was such a good thing for a bank and school to do. When we moved I had $33.00 in my account. Bonnie had in the $40's and Ron had in the $20's. I recall it was almost $100.00 between us. Dad said he was taking it and buying a heifer at the Saturday sale in Caldwell. He told us he would pasture it through the summer and fall then sell her in the late fall so we could get the increased money. How excited the three of us were about this! This turned out to be the first of many unfulfilled promises dad would give. That fall dad sold "Sue" our name for the heifer. We never heard one thing about the money just like all the other later promises would be.

It wasn't a surprise for the oldest brothers and sisters to hear about dad's promises to us kids that would almost always go unfulfilled. They had it happen to them every year. I didn't know this until we were in our early teens and would talk with the older siblings. One particular summer when I was in early high school dad promised us five kids $50.00/each for hoeing the beets for the summer. We would have $250.00 total to spend. All of us but Rich were going to use our money to buy school clothes. All through the summer we were so glad to come in for lunch from the field so we could devour the Sears catalog looking for the best buys and what we really loved. Every day we would make changes until we were finally ready to place our orders the early part of August. Just like all other times, we were told the money wasn't there so we would need to let mom buy some material at the local store in Homedale, Idaho and make our clothes. Mom went into Homedale with her $20.00 and bought flannel for Ron's and my two shirts each and some material for a couple dresses each for Bonnie and Polly.

The following year Ron and I decided we were not going to let this happen again. We decided to buy 300 baby chicks. We had an abandoned little house on our place that we fenced. We kept the baby chicks in the house under lights until they were older and then we put them out in the yard. By the end of July they were big enough for butchering. I called our neighbors to see if they wanted to buy freshly cleaned chickens. They were between 3.5 and 4 pounds. I couldn't believe how quickly they sold. Every day after lunch we'd set up a table in the yard outside the house. We'd boil the water, kill 25-30 chickens, dip them in the boiling water so we could pluck them. Afterwards we'd take them in the house to clean them. We'd then put them in our freezer overnight and deliver them to the neighbor the next day. We sold all the chickens within a couple weeks and kept 30 hens for mom to have new laying hens. Mom helped us every day with our work. This time we had our money and so when we devoured the Sears catalog, we made the order. The surprise in it was for mom. A lady in the department store in Homedale was mom's size. I drove in and asked her what size she wore so I could order mom a dress from the catalog. She knew mom so told me what size. Ron and I picked out a dress we thought was "perfect" for her. When the order came a couple weeks later we eagerly opened it and there was mom's dress. We pulled it out and held it up. We told mom to come in the living room where we were doing our unpacking. When she saw the dress she asked, "What's this? We told her it was for her for all the work she did helping us. Her response was priceless!

"Oh, you silly boys, you." She said. This was her line when she was overcome or without words. The look on her face will be one I'll cherish the rest of my life.

Our farm was 120 acres with about 90 of them irrigated and farmed. The other 30 were above the ditch line so irrigation water couldn't reach them. The 30 acres weren't dramatically high in elevation compared to the other 90, but at our young age we thought they were rugged mountains. Knowing about Mt. Whitney and Mt. McKinley being the United States' highest peaks, we quickly named these two mounds as such. Our first goals were to run to the top of them without needing to stop for a breather. The next goal was to ride the bike down one without crashing. We even had a homemade go-cart which we tried riding down Mt. Whitney. We didn't fare so well with that attempt! About once a year I take a drive by our old farm and reminisce. I realize just how distorted our thinking can be at young ages regarding the size of something.

A year or two into our farming days brought out the stories from my older siblings regarding their days on the farm by Homedale. There were lots of similarities. Things like the beets needed to be weeded all summer long so who did that hoeing? It was always us kids with mom. Dad always seemed to have something else he needed to go do. Hay hauling usually found dad's help. He was a strong man and this work took much strength throwing the hay bales on the wagon and stacking them. I well remember the day we got a hay elevator to assist stacking the bales by the cow manger. Later we were able to get an elevator that attached to the hay wagon and it elevated the bales alongside the wagon so we only had to grab them off for stacking purposes. The nice part about stacking hay was it ended with each cutting of hay. The sad thing about hoeing the beet fields was that it never ended. A day never passed but what we were either in the field hoeing or knowing we should be. Most farmers hired farm worker crews to come and do this. Not dad, he fathered his own crew.

In the early 60's the game show Password came to television. We loved watching it and I got the brilliant idea of using a dictionary to get words we put on little pieces of paper. We'd carry the words to the beet field and play the game while we hoed rows and rows throughout the hot afternoon summer days. We would even play this at times in the evening after the cows were milked and the last of the water "was set". This is a term used for the irrigation being done in the crop fields. I'll never forget the time playing Password in the evening when

I was dad's partner. The word was "lock". I started the clues with saying--paddle. Dad, of course, went right to boat. Ron was mom's partner and I don't recall what he said, but we couldn't get dad or mom from the initial thinking of boat or canoe. Finally after giving the 10 clues we could give we said the word was "lock".

Dad spouted, "where in the world did you come up with paddle!?"

I said, "from the word "paddlelock".

He retorted, "Good grief, don't you know the word is padlock and not "paddlelock"? Actually, at the age of 10 I didn't know that. Lucky for me the issue ended there. On other occasions, with the game being as innocent as this one, if dad got upset or he lost due to something one of us did, you could expect one of his severe beatings.

The work on the farm wasn't absent of tractor work. This was something my brother Ron looked forward to. He was mechanical like dad and many of my brothers. I was a farmer with a shovel or a hoe. I did share the tractor work, but if it was a choice between Ron or me, I'd ask him to take the tractor and I'd do the irrigating. I wasn't scared of the tractor, but I was very scared of what dad would do to me if I damaged it or damaged the equipment being pulled by the tractor. I wasn't adept to knowing how to fix a problem that would arise. As I grew older, for some reason, I did love to do the combining. I also enjoyed driving the grain trucks to town loaded with wheat or barley. This was probably more about the freedom doing this provided. When we had to overhaul a tractor or truck engine, which we did a number of times, dad would always express his disgust when I couldn't recall what had been done the time before. Each time we did an overhaul was like the first time for me. HIs line for me as I got into high school was, "Good grief, if it doesn't have a musical note beside it you don't know what to do with it!" Even that line didn't make sense to me. For, although I sang, I couldn't read notes. I think he equated singing to reading notes.

Some of the most enjoyable parts of our farm life were our fishing trips. Dad did love to fish and so did all of us kids. I think some of the pleasure was sheer happiness getting away from the work for a few hours and enjoying goofing around. Dad would never go fishing if he were in a bad mood so this was always a predictable time for dad. Most commonly we would go to the Snake River which was only a few miles down the road. We had a few "favorite spots" where we could always predict success. These fishing trips were also great experiences when company would come. Whether it was a sibling of my parents or one of the older kids and their family, we would cherish these moments. A favorite was a time when our Aunt Vee and Uncle John came with our cousin Shirley. All of us went to the river and caught between 30-40 catfish. That night mom had a huge fish fry fixing enough for 10 hungry fishermen. When supper was done and we boys had to go milk the cows, there were about six or seven fish left on the platter. After milking, about one and a half hours, we came back in the house. Aunt Vee was just finishing the last fish on the platter. We said, "Aunt Vee, did you eat all of those catfish?" Her response was priceless. She said, "Boys, there are a few things in life that are more important than an appetite. I don't eat catfish because I'm hungry, I eat them because I love them and there are still some on the platter. Now that they are all gone, I'm done." Ron and I have laughed at that statement many times.

CHAPTER 5

Abuse on the Farm

The beatings on the farm were a change from the ones in California. Dad now had milking hoses to add to the whipping tools. On one particular day, dad and mom were going to the sale in Caldwell. We had gotten a 10 gallon can of dirty milk back that morning and dad wasn't happy. I believe it was Ron who asked if we kids could go fishing at the Snake River while they were gone. Dad's response was, "What do you think?" We all agreed that he didn't say no so we took the pickup and went to the river. Rich drove as he was the only one licensed to do so. When dad returned and saw that we had gone fishing he took one of the milking hoses, equivalent to a 1" thick garden hose, and began to give each of us boys a whipping. This may have been one time we deserved it--just not so severely.

Rich's sexual abuse changed as we got to the farm. Instead of him having an orchard to take me to, he now came to my bed at night. This brought about a different issue because Ron and I slept in the same bed. Even though Ron was never bothered, he would sometimes awaken when Rich was "doing his thing" to me. By now, ages 10 & 11, both Ron and I knew this was wrong and needed to stop. I decided the right thing to do was to tell dad. This would surely end it once and for all. The day I told dad was a Monday. I remember this because each Monday was the day mom would sterilize the milking equipment washing all of the hoses and buckets with boiling water. The equipment would be hung in the utility room off the kitchen for drying until Monday night's milking time.

After telling dad that Rich was coming to my bed and doing some things to me, I don't recall what I said exactly, dad pulled Rich into the utility room and began the beating. I distinctly recall seeing the milking equipment in the room. I sat outside the room rolled into a fetal position listening to Rich's screams, moans and groans while dad continued the beating and slugging. I covered my ears but I couldn't hush the wails. When it finally ended, dad came out first and looked at me. He said, "He doesn't get it." I had no idea what he meant by that. I don't know if I went into the room at that point or if Rich walked out. It doesn't really matter, it was Rich's appearance that is permanently embedded in my mind. His face was unrecognizable. It was a mass of blood. I stood in horror. I had caused this to happen to him. Of all the beatings I'd witnessed or experienced, none equaled this. The horrible part is that within two weeks Rich was back at his visits to my bed. Now, however, I did not know what to do. I would never, ever tell dad again. I couldn't again cause anyone to get what Rich had received. But, what do I do? This was a big question for someone only 10 or 11.

My sister Bonnie was by now a young teenager. She was interested in "looking pretty" each day as she went to school. Dad was opposed to anything a girl might wish to do to accentuate her beauty. Bonnie wasn't to rat her hair (a big thing in the 60's!). She was also not to wear any makeup. We had a long driveway to walk in order to catch the bus each morning. I volunteered to be her helper--her "knight in shining armor". As we'd get far enough away from the house I'd hold the mirror she kept in her purse so she could do the necessary ratting of hair and apply the desired makeup. These practices lasted throughout her junior high and high school years. I was in later elementary when we started this. If a brother could be in love with his sister, I was. I thought she was beautiful and if I could help this, I would do whatever it took to defend and support her. As we got older we had decided when she graduated from high school she'd work for two years so we could go to college together. She graduated from high school and immediately went to college without waiting. I knew this was the right thing for her to do but my "brother's heart" was a tad bit broken.

As close as Bonnie and I were, I never had told her about Rich's use of me. I'm sure there are deep-seated reasons for this somehow connected to the shame I was feeling deep within. It wasn't until I went into three years of counseling and PTSD therapy in my late 50's that I finally told her about it. She and I cried together as I walked the "path of telling" with her. She had many questions most of which I couldn't answer.

By the age of 12 to 13 I was beginning to know the "sinfulness" of Rich's behaviors with me. Around the age of 12 I had given my heart to Jesus at a revival our little Free Methodist Church in Adrian was hosting. It was a Thursday night and for some reason I was the only one of the kids who had gone with mom and dad. When the evangelist asked if anyone wanted to come to the altar to ask Jesus into their heart my mom simply placed her hand on my shoulder. My heart was already pounding so I immediately went forward and prayed the simple prayer of a child. I recall knowing Christ was now in my heart. What I began to wonder was why with Christ in my heart did Rich keep doing what he was doing? This was a question never spoken out loud.

With my own onset of puberty looming I was beginning to have many mixed emotions. I saw my body beginning to develop as Rich's already had. I couldn't help but wonder if that meant I would do the same things? The thing I found so disgusting and most confusing was the fact there were times when the abuse by now felt stimulating. I didn't act on that, but I couldn't figure out what I was to do with all these confusing emotions. Because Ron and I still shared a bed, he was still aware at times of Rich's visits. One time he even asked me why I was the only one chosen? I think in Ron's mind this was just something Rich did. He had no idea the awful confusion and shame it was causing me. I never ever talked about any of this to anyone. At the age of 16 Ron and I made a plan to stop this. He agreed that the next time Rich came to our bed he would turn on the bedroom light since he slept right under it and I would pull out the shovel handle I had placed between the mattress and springs of our bed. It wasn't long until we completed this action. Rich came, Ron and I awakened, Ron turned on the light and I pulled the shovel handle out. With this I immediately got out of bed and pulled the shovel handle over Rich's head telling him I would kill him if he ever touched me again. This threat finally stopped once and for all his abusive acts.

CHAPTER 6

School

I was entering 4th grade when we moved to the farm in Oregon. My first year was in a little country school where 3rd, 4th and 5th graders were with one teacher--Mrs. Cunningham. Ron was in third, I was in fourth so the two of us were together. Bonnie was in 6th so with another teacher. Polly's birthday wasn't until December. The school started her but felt she needed another year before she was able to be at school all day. Rich was 19 by now so mom and dad never enrolled him. He had completed his 9th grade year in Escondido. He was able to do some reading and some simple math.

There were six students in Ron's and my class with Mrs. Cunningham. She was an energetic teacher and I loved this about her. The school being so small, it had no lunch program so we took our sack lunches each day. Ron and I would usually sit together while eating. Mrs. Cunningham asked one day if we took giggle pills for breakfast? I guess that characteristic was deeply embedded in our genes.

Starting my fifth grade year the Ridgeview school closed and was annexed into Adrian, Oregon. It was funny to me hearing the kids talk about going to a big school. My word, we had moved from Escondido where there were several hundred students in a grade to having only 6 students in 3 grades. Moving to Adrian where we had one class for a grade was nothing. The class had 36 students in it, but I didn't see that as a problem either. This fifth grade teacher became the one adult who God used to fashion the stage for my career path in life. Mrs. Anna Long was her name. She was serious and focused as a teacher, but I never felt she was mean. There is a huge difference between those two characteristics. She truly wanted her kids to learn and I've always been an eager learner. I also had a focusing problem getting started. If someone is beside me I've always thought I needed to talk to them. That gene also runs deep in me!

This 5th grade year I watched Mrs. Long take kids from non-reading to actually reading independently. She was relentless in her work. I found myself drawn to her instructional ways and the success of them. Even though some kids felt she was "mean" because she kept them in at recess to complete work, I found her fascinating because the staying in accomplished successful readers. I was so enthralled by this I wanted to spend my life being just like her. A cute story about her for me is the one of the many times she had kids stay in from morning recess to work on their reading. One of my friends was kept in so I stayed to be of assistance to him. Mrs. Long had stepped out of the room for a moment, probably to use the restroom, and I was with my friend. He wouldn't focus on his work and I was frustrated with him. Just as I said a "bad word" to him because he wouldn't focus, Mrs. Long stepped into the room. She heard me and quietly came up alongside of me. She whispered in my ear, "I never thought I'd hear a word like that from a fine, young man like you." Well, I guess you know I made a firm decision right then and there she would never hear something like that from me again. Along with that, no one else would either! Mrs. Long had spoken!

Adrian School system had two buildings, an elementary/junior high and the high school. They were a stone's throw apart and still are today. As I worked my way through the remaining elementary/junior high years I continued to love school. I never saw myself as smart, but I did know I wanted to learn all I could about a lot of things. I'm told I asked a lot of questions but that was because I was curious. I never equated curiosity at that time with any level of intelligence. The crippling verbal abuse of dad was taking hold by now. It was my freshman year in high school that I stumbled into wondering, "Am I smart?"

At some point in junior high, when we got to go to the library regularly, I fell in love with the magazine, "Boy's Life". It had great articles as well as some interesting advertisements in the back. There were ads for stamp collecting from HE Harris Co. The ad said they would send stamps "on approval" and it didn't cost you anything! I had heard of stamp collecting and coin collecting, but to have my own? Wow! I ordered some of those free stamps "on approval". Once getting them I found out what the "on approval" meant. The part I don't recall is where I got the money to buy some of these. It had to have been from mom, but the memory isn't there. By my freshman year in high school I had an album and a good start with the collection. All throughout high school I spent much of my home time, particularly Sunday afternoons, working on this. One of the stamps I got in the many $1.00 bags I'd buy of assorted stamps was rather valuable. Estimates were in the hundreds of dollars. I sort of felt rich! When I graduated from high school I gave this album to my brother Ron. Ron was the one who would get stuck with work I'd miss when I was singing so I thought this would "pay him back" for never complaining about this.

After the first 9 weeks of my freshman year, I got my report card. I was stunned to see that I had all A's and B's and I was being recommended to think about National Honor Society. Good grief, that organization was only for the smart ones. Did this mean I could qualify for that? I couldn't join it until my sophomore year and then only as a junior member, but it was quietly exciting for me. I certainly didn't ask any questions about it because of dad's criticisms. He'd say things like, "Oh, you just think you are smarter than anyone else" or "You just think you're too good for anyone else." No I didn't! In fact, I often asked questions thinking I needed to know what everyone else already seemed to know. I always felt like I was a step or two behind them and I needed to catch up if I were ever to be successful.

The other thing dad would often say to me was, "I need to kill that spirit of yours." I had heard this for as long as I could remember. It left me knowing my spirit was bad and I needed to do my best to hide it or squelch it somehow. I had a longing to please dad, but I only seemed to get farther and farther away from this goal.

My freshman year I could take two electives. There were only two offered so I took them: Ag and choir. Ag was a stretch for me in some ways, it was a lot like working with dad at home, except dad was never there and I found some of the things I could do. We welded, soldered, did woodworking and more. I actually won the regional tool identification contest. I probably didn't know what to do with half of them, but I did know all of them quickly by name.

It was in choir that God opened a huge door for me. Our choir director was new to Adrian that year. She was a rather large lady named Mrs. Denman. She had gray hair so I knew she was "old". Later I found out she was only 33 years old and had two young children. My mom was in her 50's by now and wasn't yet gray so I just thought if you were gray, you were older.

Mrs. Denman came to me in early November of 1964 and asked if I'd consider singing the last verse of "Silent Night" for the Christmas program that year. I was shocked! She wanted me to sing a solo--in front of people? I had done a little of this when I was younger, but I hadn't sung for anyone since that first grade year in Escondido and a little for Christmas programs in our church. This seemed like a big deal and I sure didn't think I was capable of it. However, she said she would work with me if I'd come to the choir room during lunch time. This in and of itself was motivation enough to say, "Yes!" Mrs. Denman was never to know during these high school years about Rich, but the offer to not be with the crowd during lunch was totally freeing for me. By this time I was scared to death of anyone being too close to me, touching me, rubbing shoulders, legs inadvertently touching while sitting by anyone. The abuse of Rich was taking its toll. Being free of this was huge.

I began coming to the music room daily. I sang the solo for the school's program that Christmas. Amazing to me was the fact that afterwards, people from our church and other churches started asking if I'd come and sing for them. My sophomore year in high school, Mrs. Denman entered me in the Oregon's regional solo contest. This would be taking place in LaGrande, Oregon at Eastern Oregon College of Education. I didn't understand this request as a chance for me to be judged for quality of singing. I was OK with it if she wanted. She asked dad and he even said yes to it. She lived in Ontario and drove all the way to our farm south of Adrian, 30 miles each way, to pick me up, go to LaGrande, and take me home afterwards. I could have never dreamed in my wildest imagination what would take place from attending this event. I tied for first place. I didn't know this at first. Mrs. Denman and I were driving home from LaGrande, a 120 mile drive, when she asked me how I felt I had done. I didn't have any idea what a report card for singing looked like. I said, well, if it were a class I probably got a "C" thinking I'd probably done average. Her first words were, "I thought that's what you'd say." She went onto tell me I had tied for first place. In fact, the judges had awarded me first place but then they had discovered the tenor who had won the state contest a year ago from Pendleton was singing and I would be placed ahead of him. So, they said we tied for first and he would be the one going to state later that spring. She then gave me the rating sheet and I was simply stunned to read the complimentary things written on it. I'd never had anything written about me like that before.

Mrs. Denman and I became a pair. I was in the choir room after this not only at noon times but whenever I had 10 or more minutes. We were constantly working on new songs and she was continuously creating new places for me to sing. My junior and senior years in high school took me to the state solo contests where I won first place for Oregon State in the tenor division. Along with this she opened the door for me to attend All Northwest in Missoula, Montana for an entire week. This took an act of God! She had sent in a tape of my singing and I was accepted. But, I had to ask dad if I could be gone for a week. I just couldn't do that. So, she drove out to our farm and told dad herself. I've never known to this day what she said to him or what all he said to her. It wasn't until the next day at school I found out from her that he'd said I could go. This probably sounds quite dysfunctional for a home, but it was a very normal action for ours.

In all of this Mrs. Denman never put me on the spot asking about my home. She'd sometimes ask me, "A penny for your thoughts?" I'd always respond, "What?" That would be the end of the conversation.

Mrs. Denman along with a couple other teachers at Adrian High got me involved in leadership activities. In fact, it was my 8th grade teacher, my first male teacher, who was first to direct me in this path. While we were studying American History, he divided us into two parties: Tories and Whigs. Each party was to nominate their presidential candidate and the two candidates were to campaign. We then had an election mirroring a national one. I was nominated to be the Whig presidential candidate. I didn't win the class election, but his words following the election will always stay with me. He told me to not lose heart in this loss. He knew I would make a great president someday and the only reason I had lost was due to the other candidate's popularity. Once I got to high school I quickly learned what that term meant. I never thought of myself as popular. If anyone knew about me and my abuse I wouldn't be allowed at school--I thought. However, during my high school years, I was president of Honor Society, Future Teachers of America, Junior class, and Hi-Y (a Christian youth organization). I was going to run for student body president my senior year but dad said I couldn't. He didn't want me away from the farm and this would have me too involved. In all of this, if someone would have asked me if I were a leader I would have said, "No, they just didn't have anyone else who would say yes to this." And, I would have meant that.

During my senior year Mrs. Denman thought it would be a good idea to make a record of all the festival songs I'd sung and the others I most loved. She had found a company that would make them. Over a period of several weeks, we made a reel to reel recording of about 14 songs. She sent it to the company and in the middle of June, 1968 I got a box of 125 records. I sold them for $4.25 each. That meant I got $1.00 profit for each one sold. Mrs. Denman had already done the advertising in our little community and set a date in the high school parking lot for folks to come to purchase them. I couldn't believe that all these people came to buy them. By the time fall rolled around and I started college, I had about 6 left. One of the songs on the record was a poem I'd written that she had put to music. It was titled "Only One Life". The words were:

> *There's only one life in this world we know*
> *Sometimes it's filled with sorrow and woe.*
> *There's only one way to live this life*
> *And that is with our Lord Jesus Christ.*
>
> *He'll find a way through our troubles and pain*
> *And bring us back completely whole again.*
> *So if you are troubled and life seems gone*
> *Look toward heaven, you'll see a new dawn.*

Jesus is there to carry your load
Just say, "Yes", come in Lord and you'll find treasures untold
This may not bring much meaning to you
But it brightens each day as I say it through.

This poem means more to me today than it did at the age of 16 when I first wrote it.

How many teachers have you known who would take such an interest in a student? Yet, I was the recipient of all this. How much I thank God for her part in my early life.

Mrs. Denman and I remained in contact all through my life until her death two years ago, 2013. I had been able to share with her my testimony and just how significant she was for me. During my high school years I would likely have ended it all for me if it hadn't been for her. God used her in powerful ways to not only save my life, but to give me a life-long use of music and leadership.

Her two children asked if I'd come to Portland, Oregon for her funeral service and sing. I said I would. My wife and I drove there giving me a chance to tell my wife Kathy, just how unsettled I was about this trip. I knew in my mind how much I had robbed their mom during my high school years. They were in early elementary at that time and I having been a parent knew how much time kids want to be with their parents. Their mom was carting me all over the place instead of being with them.

After the funeral service in the Catholic church Mrs. Denman attended, there was a wonderful lunch put together for the family. I was asked to stay for it which reluctantly I said we would. It was there I was stunned to begin to hear what the two children began to share with me. They each had their own children, one had three and the other had four. They shared with me that I was they and their children's legend. Each year they played the record of my singing which their mom and I had made of my competition songs as well as several others. Mrs. Denman would tell them about her student who, in spite of many barriers, went on to win many awards and become a college graduate. She would use me to motivate her children and her grandchildren that nothing is impossible with God. I simply started crying when they were sharing all of this with me. Little did I know that my life could be a motivation for anyone, when for me it had needed to be "TOP SECRET". It is just amazing how God takes a mess and makes it a message. (A quote from the work of Celebrate Recovery). I told them just how much their mom had meant to me and without her I likely wouldn't be here today. Now I stay in touch with the two kids. They actually played the record this winter again for everyone. The grandkids are now passing the story on to their young kids about grandma and a student she had many years ago.

There is one more thing Mrs. Denman taught me in the line of wisdom that I've never forgotten and have tried to use routinely throughout my life. I had come into the music room one morning telling her about someone who had told me I should.... I can't even remember now what it was I was told. I was upset with the person for "interfering" with something I didn't think was any of his business. However, Mrs. Denman's response has stuck in my memory like gorilla glue. She said, "You know, one should never judge wisdom by its carrier. Some of the finest wisdom can be lost if you don't consider it. The carrier can be used by God and you will miss it if you judge the person ahead of listening to their words." I have used this many times over my life.

High School is usually when dating takes a front seat. Well, for dad's kids, it was front in our thinking, but could never materialize. As long as we lived under dad's roof, we were not going to date anyone. This was one of the things that had caused my older siblings to begin some of their rebellion. I knew all of this so I just didn't press the subject. To be brutally honest, I was scared to death of dating. I just didn't know how I could overcome having someone sitting right next to me, wanting to hug me, touch me and some other things.... In response, I was to do that too with them! I'll talk more about this as we get to college.

My junior year I was class president. This is the year where the high school prom is hosted by the junior class. Thus, I was not only to organize our meetings putting the event together, I was also to MC the night which meant I would need a date. There was a sweet, very smart, Japanese girl in my class named Gay. She was shy and quiet. I asked her if she'd be my date. I maneuvered around dad telling him I had to have a date due to being class president. He didn't object to that. Gay and I were probably something you'd want to watch as a comedy nowadays. When I got to her house I was met with this lovely girl wearing a spaghetti strap gown. This was 1967 so wrist corsages weren't invented yet. So, I was to pin her corsage onto the strap. My hands were like ice and I had to touch the strap to pin it on her. I even had to touch her skin which even as I write this makes my neck and back TIGHT. I'm sure she thought she had Adrian's worst LOSER that night. She sat by the passenger door of dad's car and I drove. I don't recall even a word we may have spoken or if we even did speak. I just recall collapsing onto the steering wheel when I was driving away from her home wondering what in the world was I ever going to do?

45

My class in high school had 36 students in it. We all knew each other quite well. There were the popular ones, and those who weren't. I never knew where I fit in this arena. Actually, I didn't give it too much thought. My friends tended to be what I'd now call the underdogs. I've always had a heart for them. One friend in particular was named Mike. I knew he was kind of different, but to some degree, who wasn't? My sis Bonnie told me to be careful around him because she thought he was gay. My brother Ron would say the same thing but I would just blow them off saying they were critical like everyone else. My wakeup came early in my senior year. Mike had volunteered to be the football team's helper. I was staying after school one day in the fall because Mrs. Denman was taking me to an event for which I was singing. We would leave about an hour after school was out. Mike asked me to go to the locker rooms and help him do the laundry. We got the washers going when he wanted me to undress. I told him I sure wouldn't. He said he wanted to show me something. I backed away from him as he took his pants down. He said he wanted me to know he could get an erection which was satisfactory in size in spite of what the coaches had teased him about. I had heard the coaches tormenting remarks but I didn't need anything like this. I ran upstairs to the music room and waited for Mrs. Denman to leave with me. This only reinforced in my mind that ones like Mike and Rich saw something in me making them think I was easy prey for them. I needed to always be on high alert for this.

As I got into my senior year I was deeply into activities, singing, classes and anything else I could do that kept me busy. I never wanted a lax moment and most of the time I didn't have any. This, of course, was only for the school time hours. I still had to go home every day on the bus to milk cows with

Ron and Rich. I was getting closer to my goal however and at moments, I could see the end of the tunnel. When I had begun high school I was so burdened with home life and how much I was hiding, I figured out how many days I needed to endure in order to have the freedom high school graduation would provide. I started counting my days backwards starting at 1460 knowing this would someday come to any end.

An unusual, yet very touching thing happened for me at the beginning of my senior year. By now Mrs. Denman had grown the music program at Adrian to have half the student body in the choir. Two sophomore guys, Steve and Earl, both tenors, joined the choir. The odd thing to me was that they wanted to sit beside me. More than that, they wanted me to be their friend. Both of them were jocks in all the sports of the school. I saw myself as anything but this and I certainly wasn't worth their time and effort. However, they were relentless in everyday sitting beside me, questioning me about much in school, leadership roles I played and how to do this or that. To be honest with you, I would go home nightly and cry with thanks for God giving me these two friends. I had always been drawn to the underdog. I know now much of this was due to my self-esteem. However, these two seemed to be drawn to me and I could not figure out what I had to offer them. All I knew is that I was thankful for this tremendous gift of friendship from these two misguided souls. Their friendship grew beyond choir to much about our lives. I helped them with their leadership campaigns. They thought I had influence in the student body. My goodness, I thought, where did this thinking of theirs come from? I sure couldn't let them know what this friend truly consisted of.

Something happened my senior year that changed me permanently connected to my Senior English teacher, Mrs. Dilly. Mrs. Dilly was the high school librarian as well as the main English teacher. For the first nine weeks that year she had assigned me to read <u>Gone with the Wind</u>. This book had 900+ pages. I had read a little prior to this, but this seemed overwhelming. I wasn't one to contest what a teacher told me so I undertook the assignment. However, as the nine weeks drew to a close I had only read 80-90 pages. I did my best to write a report on the book scanning the last 20 or so pages so I could include something about the conclusion of the book. I turned the report in and three days later came to Mrs. Dilly to confess my "lie". She said, "Do you think I didn't know this already? I've been waiting to see if you'd come and tell me." She went on to say that my assignment was still the same. I needed in the next 9 weeks to read <u>Gone with the Wind</u>. This time I read it cover to cover. All of a sudden I began to see what rich literature was really like and I loved it. I'll never forget the one day in class, I had finished my assignment and had pulled the book out to read until class ended. I got to the part where Melanie died. I was trying to not be conspicuous but was struggling to hold back my own tears of sadness. Mrs. Dilly must have been watching as she came to my side and whispered, "What happened?" I told her Melanie just died! She patted my back and said, "I understand."

After <u>Gone with the Wind,</u> Mrs. Dilly assigned me <u>An American Tragedy</u>. I read it with fervor. It was over 1,000 pages but now I had commitment and didn't count pages. I only counted the minutes until I could get back to the good book I was reading. If you are unfamiliar with the book, a young lad of meager means works his way through poverty to go to college. He dates a girl and gets her pregnant. To cover this up he drowns her which eventually leads to his lifelong demise. I was shocked with what this kid had done. I asked Mrs. Dilly why she wanted me to read this. She said she wanted me to be ready to step into the world and not get swallowed up with what the world could do to me. I assured her I would never do such a thing. However, I know now Mrs. Dilly was much wiser than I had thought. I was right in that I'd never take another person's life, but learning about the "pull of the world" was something I knew little about and greatly appreciated what she was wanting me to learn from this.

Being a Free Methodist I had always envisioned myself going to Seattle Pacific University. It was one of our denomination's schools and it had a great reputation for medical and educational majors. I made my application early and started completing as many scholarship applications as I could find. I knew there wouldn't be any financial help from my parents. I had done their taxes the past couple years and I knew first-hand how little they actually made by farming. In fact, if it weren't for the milk checks that came every two weeks, I didn't know how we lived. I knew I was going to be a teacher, thanks to Mrs. Long's 5th grade modeling and God's leading. So, SPU was to be the perfect match for me.

The spring of that year my dad actually loaded three of us into our car and took us to Seattle for senior days at the college. One of them was a girl I was graduating from high school with and went to the Free Methodist church in Adrian. The other one was a girl from Nyssa or Ontario. I had cousins in Seattle and their two daughters close to my age were going to SPU. I was going to sing for a scholarship while there and one of their daughters was playing for me. She and I were to meet an hour ahead of the audition at the music building on campus. We arrived late Friday night and the audition was 1:00 Saturday afternoon. Being a country boy, left-handed who always got his directions turned around (left being right and vise versa), I left the dorm I stayed in early for the music building. I had been given good directions I was told. The campus is hilly and very wooded. Leaving the dorm, I was immediately lost. The map in hand was Greek to me. I started asking people for directions to the music building. They would kindly direct me and the moment they were gone I was just as lost. Instead of getting to the building an hour ahead of the audition, I arrived 3 minutes ahead. Sharon, my cousin, and I had no time to practice. We simply went to the audition room and were almost immediately called to perform. For whatever reason, the audition seemed to go fine. I got the scholarship, but, I knew I would never be able to attend this university. I would be lost getting to every class every day! I came home feeling totally lost and disillusioned. What was I to do now that my dreams were shattered?

On Monday I shared my dilemma with my good friend Jim. He told me he was going the following week to the senior days at Northwest Nazarene College which was in Nampa, ID, an hour drive from our homes. I asked him why I had never heard of it and he said likely because I wasn't Nazarene. I knew enough about the denomination to know they were very similar to Free Methodists, but that was about it. I quickly did what little research I could about it. I found they also had a strong education department as well as music. I could also apply for a music scholarship with them. I went to their senior days the following weekend. To my great relief I could see the education building and the music buildings from the dorm. The campus was flat! What a silly thing to praise God about, but for me

I was ecstatic. I applied for a scholarship there and got it. It wasn't as good of one at SPU, but I was also able to get a couple other scholarships, grants and loans to complete the other costs. I WAS GOING TO COLLEGE.

The little Adrian Free Methodist church was really struggling by the time I was a senior. We were losing a really good pastor and his replacement was going to quickly drive away most of the ones left attending. It closed and our family started attending a Free Methodist church in Idaho, closer to Caldwell. Its name is Deer Flat Free Methodist. It was huge compared to our 25-30 people. On any given Sunday they would have about 200 people. Their youth group had 30-40 youth and I quickly made acquaintances with some of them. The pastor had me sing on Sunday mornings rather often and I felt important there. I was asked to sing in the cantata they were preparing for Easter. About February, I started driving over to the church on Sunday evenings for the practices. I had several solos in it because I was given the part of Jesus.

That Easter Sunday of 1968 Mom had invited a brother, Ralph and his family to come for Easter dinner. He had three kids and we all loved having them come. At dinner that day Ralph began to tease dad about a speech issue he sometimes had saying "twigger" for trigger and "electwicity" for electricity. Dad quickly denied he did any such thing. Mom and I reinforced what Ralph was saying and all of us were rather laughing about this. This practice was common in our house--picking on someone's weak point. Dad wasn't going to find any humor in it so we dropped the subject.

Ralph went home later in the afternoon with his family and immediately upon his departure dad came to mom and me saying, "You sure know how to make a man feel like a heel!

Saying, I can't say electricity or trigger--I can say them if I want too!" I said, "Dad, we weren't doing anything you don't do, it was just in fun." He assured mom and me there was no fun in it for him.

That evening I started the milking a little early as I needed to be at church for the Easter production of the cantata, No Greater Love. As I finished the milking and came through the living room to the bathroom dad asked where I thought I was headed. I told him I was getting ready to leave for Deer Flat for the Easter cantata. He told me, "You are not going anywhere."

I said, "Dad, we've been practicing this for months and I have the solos of Jesus."

He said, "You can rattle on all you want but you are not going anyplace."

I went to the phone to call the church which was long distance from our place in Oregon. As I was dialing dad came over and grabbed the phone out of my hand slamming the receiver down on its holder. He said, "You are not going any place and you are not calling anyone."

I stood up glaring at him and said, "All my life you have talked about being a decent person and making good decisions. Now you are telling me I can't go to the production when I have the lead part?" Once again he reminded me I could say whatever I wanted but wasn't going any place or calling anyone. With this, he stormed out of the house driving away in the car and taking the keys out of the pickup so I couldn't go in it either.

I ran downstairs to our bedroom sobbing. I eventually wrote a letter to my brother Herb in southern California asking if I could come and live with him as soon as I graduated from high school and work there until NNC started in the fall. After writing the letter I came up stairs and mom asked me what I was doing. I told her about the letter and she asked me to wait three days before mailing it. If I still felt the same, go ahead and put it in the mailbox. Mom never offered too much advice but when she did I highly respected it. I waited the three days and tore the letter up.

The day after Easter I went into the principal's office of our high school. I told him enough about what had taken place the day before and I desperately needed to call the pastor of Deer Flat. It was long distance from the high school, but he let me call anyway. Pastor Jim actually answered the phone. I tried my best to politely tell him how sorry I was for not showing the evening before. He was so thoughtful and only said, "It's ok Earnie. I know your dad and understand." At that point I really didn't know what he knew about dad, but I really appreciated his attitude with me.

Even though I was told dad was proud of my singing, he never indicated any such attitude with me. The spring of my junior year when I first won the Oregon state solo contest, he actually got mad at me saying I would now get "the big head" and wouldn't want to have anything to do with the family. It took two to three weeks for him to even treat me civilly. I did all I could to try and be whatever pleased him to prove I was still the same boy. Interestingly, when I won again the spring of my senior year, dad said, "Well, last year I thought you were lucky, maybe not." That was as close to a compliment as dad ever gave me during his life.

As a senior at Adrian I was graduating mid-May, 1968. A couple weeks ahead of graduation I was asked by a neighboring farmer if I could work for him through the summer. His farm was only about three miles down the road from ours. He would give me a Honda 90 cycle to ride for irrigating and to travel from home to work each day. I needed to be there by 7:00 am and would get home about 7:00 pm at night. My biggest concern was that Ron and Rich would have all the milking to do at home and all the farm labor to do. However, Ron was very supportive and said that was fine with him. When graduation rolled around everyone was in the partying mood. However, my excitement was that I was going to work the next day and it wouldn't have to be with dad. I went home and started what I thought would be my journey to freedom the next day.

The summer of 1968 I worked three months and three weeks straight never taking a single day off. I'd go to church on Sunday and then hop on the cycle to go move sprinkler lines and do all the irrigating. Joe Nelson, the farmer, was renting many farms in the area and I was one of two irrigators for him. His wife Donna would fix lunch for her family and me each day. I was quite taken back seeing how casual they were with one another, offering compliments, laughing with one another, yelling at one another at times, yet, no one ever blew like dad would. I was glad to know life didn't need to be as my home had always been. At the end of the summer Joe surprised me with a bonus. He was paying me $300.00 a month for my work which I thought was very substantial already. When he gave me my end of season check, he also gave me a brand new portable typewriter. It was Smith Corona's latest model. On top of that--it was blue! I typed about 80 words a minute so I knew I could use it to make money in college typing term papers for others. I was one grateful lad!

My last week before heading to college I spent at home. It was mid September so Ron and Polly were in school during the day. I would primarily have the day with mom because dad was doing his own work. I took mom shopping with me so she could help me buy an iron and ironing board, laundry stuff and all the toiletries I'd need. I got school supplies for my room as well as bedding for my bed. It was really nice to have this special time with mom. I had asked mom to not iron my clothes that summer because I wanted to know how to do it myself. With the singing I did I needed ironed dress shirts and pants so I would look nice. She accommodated this and showed me how to press the collars of shirts as well as all the other secrets of ironing shirts and pants so the creases were in the right places.

On Friday of this last week I was to head to NNC and get my room in the dorm. Student activities were to begin that night. That particular day dad left taking the car keys and the pickup keys so I couldn't leave for college. Why he did this I will never know. I suppose I may find this out when I get to heaven and he opens up with this news. Mom never learned to drive, but for some reason she had a key to the car. So, she, Rich and I loaded my things into the back seat and trunk and left for Nampa where NNC would become my new home.

PART II

The Secret

College

The thought of college was for me a huge, and I mean huge, opportunity to bring fulfillment to this young man's dreams. It would be here I thought I would get grounded in my career path--being a math and science teacher, find a wife would who loved Jesus as much as I love Jesus and who wanted a family. It would be a chance to sing without the cloud of dad's ever present condemnation and judgment. There was one last thing however I was very fearful about--wetting the bed. I had never stopped wetting the bed throughout high school. The nightly wetting had ended so that I did this once every week or two, however, the fear of this in college was haunting. On July 1st, my birthday in 1968, I had turned 18 and I had wet the bed that night. The miraculous thing was that this was my last time to ever wet the bed. I learned in my adult years that bedwetting is often a body's response to stress and fear. I knew that was true for me, I just didn't know this as a young lad starting college. I prayed and prayed that God would see fit to not let this happen here.

I don't recall all the events of that first weekend at college. However, being a farm boy and having always milked cows morning and night, I was used to getting up early. I did not know the "art of sleeping in". So, my first morning I was up and at Saga--the food service provider, for breakfast at 6:00 am. Jim Langley, the friend who had told me about NNC was with me. He was also a farm boy. We were stunned to find the cafeteria didn't even open until 7:00 am. We talked about the adjustments we would need to be making here at this place and finally 7:00 came. I was going to be joining Jim and his mom going to Boise that day to do some clothes shopping for Jim. She was coming at 9:00 to pick us up. As I look back at this I always chuckle to myself. Here we were--our first step away from our homes and entering this new world thinking it operated on the time clock of the farm. We were done with breakfast by 7:20 and now had an hour and forty minutes until Jim's mom would be here. We soon acclimated to sleeping in!

The first Saturday night there were activities for the new and returning students. I don't recall what all they were, but I know I was asked to sing since I had been given a music scholarship. I don't recall what I sang, but this event led to a friendship that has sustained throughout my life. Being a math/science major I was registered to take Analytic Math & Trig as my first math course. I had taken trig my senior year at Adrian but there were only two of us taking it so we were doing it long distance through the University of Idaho. We had big fill-in-the-blank workbooks sent to us each quarter. The other student and I worked together with this. I ended with an A in trig, but actually learned very little. Thus, now that I was in this first math class, I was in over my head! I went after the first week to talk with the professor thinking he'd help just like my teachers at Adrian would assist when I asked for assistance. His only response was, "If you are stuck with this you need to transfer out into an easier class." I quickly went to my advisor and was switched to a foundation class for this one.

I've never been one to run late in anything, so the following Monday I was in my new class early to find a desk. This student came up to me and seated himself next to me. He introduced himself as Mike Benedick. He said he'd heard me sing that first weekend and wondered if I would consider being first tenor in a quartet he was wishing to start. My head was swirling with such a compliment--he wanted me? I quickly said, "Yes, I'd be happy to do this." Having been from a small church and youth group, I was unfamiliar with all the ways people sang, particularly something like a men's quartet. I say this because within a month I had been asked to sing in six others. I was quickly swamped with so many practices I could not begin to keep up. I then backed out of all of them except Mike's. He was the first to ask so I'd stay with that one.

Jim Langley and I were friends at Adrian. Yet, as we were going to college together we thought it best to get separate rooms so we could have a different roommate and with that, make new friends. This worked out well for us. His room was on the bottom floor and I was on the 3rd floor in a different wing of the dorm. I had an end room which I loved. It had windows on two walls--great place for starting plants in the winter for the next spring's garden!

My roommate was from Los Angeles, California. He was tall compared to this 5'6", 125 lb young man. He was 6' something and very outgoing. We quickly hit it off along with the two rooming across the hall from us. They were both over 6' also. I told them I felt like a toy soldier amongst the ranks of them as we'd head to Saga for meals or to the showers in the morning. They didn't seem to mind having this runty guy with them so away we went.

Gary, my roommate was very well acquainted with dating. He was right onto the girl scene upon arrival. He also knew some students since he was Nazarene and had grown up attending Nazarene functions. I didn't know anyone except Jim and Nancy. Nancy was another girl from Adrian HS and attended our church. Gary kept wanting me to join him double dating and I'd figure out some way to weasel out. He actually scared me with the things he talked about doing--kissing on the first date and then some. Good grief, I'd only had one date and that was a "door polisher" without any conversation. Gary caught on to my being so naive. He was going to break me in he said. After a few weeks he set me up with a girl who he said could teach me a few things about life and dating. She was nice, pretty and outgoing like Gary. She took me to the baseball dugout so we could have some privacy. She said she'd teach me different ways to kiss. At this point I sort of went into "overload". I recall the French kiss and that was it! My next memory is being back in the room where Gary was eagerly waiting for my responses to the night. I told him I just couldn't do all that at one time--it was too much! It scared me! He laughed and got the two across the hall. They "worked me over" saying this is what a guy is supposed to do on a date. All I knew was that if that's the case, I'd have to take it very slowly and carefully.

NNC was a conservative college in 1968. This was also into the early years of the Vietnam War. Students were wearing armbands demonstrating their resistance to the war. It was the start of the hippie movement also. These were very new terms to me--demonstrating and hippie movement--what were these things? Growing up in little Adrian kept me pretty sheltered. Also, having a dad who never let me wander out from the farm probably kept me most sheltered. I also learned I just am not attracted to this type of thing. Hippies said they wanted to be different, yet they all looked the same--that seemed like a paradox to me. Also, black armbands were almost disgusting to me. These students were saying our country was wrong. I was naive but I was a firm believer that our country was founded on the solid rock of Jesus Christ and we better be careful revolting against that. I've had to adjust my thinking in all of this, but I still believe strongly that our country is the best and closest to one honoring God.

Gary was very much a part of this rebellious movement on campus. We would talk endlessly about this. At the end of our first quarter he and about 30 others organized a dance on campus. Dancing in those days was strictly prohibited. Because he was one of the organizers for this he was expelled. He left and went to the Nazarene college in Southern California and this was the last time I ever saw him.

Jim's roommate, Bob, asked if he could move in with me at this time. Jim was wanting to have the room to himself so I said that was fine. Bob was from Emmett, Idaho and was more of a homeboy which was good for me. He lived in town but his family had a farm outside of Emmett. He took me home with him a few weekends and I was able to become acquainted with his family. Bob wanted to sing so he asked me to help him. He also played the guitar so this was kind of fun. Bob was also well acquainted with dating. He had a softer approach to "kissing". He took our broom and had me practice putting my arm around the broom handle. He said if you just put a slight bit of pressure with your hand on the shoulder of the girl and lean your body towards her she will respond and lean towards you. At that point you could turn and kiss her. By this time Mike Benedick had me double date with him and had tried to encourage me to put my arm around my date. (This water runs deep for me. My guts get tight and my shoulders get just as tight as I write this). Eventually in the spring of my freshman year, I did it! My date and I got to the girls' dorm ahead of everyone coming. I wanted to use the bench outside the dorm to try this out. We sat there on the bench for 10-15 minutes. I was struggling getting the nerve to put my arm around her. When I did I applied the little bit of pressure Bob told me about. Lo and behold, she did just as he said! She leaned towards me and I gave her a "quick peck" on the lips. All I remember from this point is running back to the boys' dorm. I ran in the room and told Bob--"I did it!" I need to add a little bit of information about this night.... I presently sing in a quartet with Mike and we often sing for assisted living homes in our area. On one occasion a couple years ago one of the ladies in the audience came up to me following the service. She introduced herself as the room mother for the girls' freshman dorm. I remembered her very well. She was funny and kind. She told me how vividly she remembered the scene out her window when I sat endlessly by a girl on the bench. She said she knew I was very nervous and she was rooting for me inside. She said it was the shortest kiss she had ever seen, but we did it! She and I both laughed a long time recalling this event!

I mentioned that Bob had been Jim's roommate the first quarter of the year. Only he and I knew about the cinnamon rolls Jim's mom would bake for him on the weekends and would send a large cookie sheet of them back to the dorm. Trust me--they were the BEST! Jim would nicely share ONE with me when he had an entire cookie sheet full of them. That winter on a Sunday night I told Bob I was going into Jim's room while he was at church. I typically went on Sunday nights, but the need to complete my plan required I stay back in the dorm. While Jim was gone I went into his room and took the cookie sheet of freshly baked rolls. I brought them to my wing and sold them for a quarter each. I then replaced the rolls with the quarters paid. Within minutes the entire cookie sheet was now covered with quarters. I returned the cookie sheet to Jim's hiding place in the closet. I warned my wing to be prepared for a tornado when Jim got home. Sure enough, Jim was soon pounding on my door and yelling loudly. He was assuring me I would soon be dead! It took a few years for him to be convinced I did a nice thing for my wing. He actually had some dollars in his wallet he hadn't had before!

My classes this freshman year were, for the most part, required ones. I was used to having all my evenings at home for homework if I needed it. On the farm there was little to do in the winter months but watch TV. That was where dad always was so I'd often stay in the kitchen doing my work. I'd even create work, like extra credit, so I'd avoid the contact. It was actually during my high school years that some of dad's verbal abuse created its deepest wounds. I didn't know it at the time, but I truly do today. Because I would avoid dad at almost any expense and would stay in the kitchen with mom he nicknamed me "Hazel". If you recall TV in the 60's, there was a program called "Hazel." Hazel was a housemaid for a family. Even when company was at our house dad would say, "Hazel, bring us ...". I would comply and he'd then say, "He's going to make someone a good wife someday." The company would laugh and so would I to not let on regarding the sting within.

My college grades took a nosedive my freshman year compared to grades in high school. I was so steeped with involvements in singing, the church I had chosen to attend and the other extra-curricular events, I took little time for studying. I did keep my grades to passing. I had to have a GPA of 2.2 to graduate in education so I did that much.

In the dorms of college there was no one but guys, of course. I hadn't even thought about what this would be like for someone who'd had 12.5 years of sexual abuse from a brother. I had just felt relieved I didn't have to worry about it anymore. However, the inner worry never left me about what someone would be thinking or if someone was lurking in the showers waiting for me when no one was around. I typically showered with the crowd so this wouldn't be the case, but once in a while I'd need to shower at less common times. On one occasion I was walking down the hall with my towel over my shoulder, butt naked. This was a common practice so I thought nothing about it. It was my winter term of the freshman year. A new guy had enrolled having come fresh out of the army. As I walked down the hall he said, "Hey Lewis, you best be careful about ever entering the service. That cute little butt of yours would be the prize for all the guys." OH MY WORD, I can't begin to tell you what that statement did to me! In those days, we had draft numbers for men entering the armed services. Mine was 91 which meant I would be drafted into the army if I weren't in college. I wasn't planning to quit, but this grounded in stone the fact I would stay in college no matter what. It also ground in stone my need to NEVER tell my story about Rich. If guys knew this they would think I was easy prey for them. MY SECRET NEEDED TO REMAIN A SECRET!

I mentioned earlier I had two windows in my dorm room. By mid January I had well over 100 plants started from seeds. These ranged from tomatoes, peppers, eggplant, geraniums and a few others that I would take home and plant in the garden and in the flower beds. However, as weeks progressed and I needed to separate the plants into their own containers, I had the guys in my wing save their milk cartons from meals and I made them the containers for the plants. Also, two window sills weren't enough room for all the plants. I quickly solicited the windows of most the rooms in my wing. I told the guys they didn't need to do anything. I'd water them. I just needed the light for the plants. Everyone obliged so I was set.

That winter session, I had Introduction to Psychology. This was a required class so the attendance in it was large--100-150 students. One particular winter day, the professor made this fatal statement, "Guys who like plants are usually gay." At first I thought that was kind of a dumb statement because most of my family is a gardening family and I didn't know anyone except Rich and the boy from high school who was like this. I had a class following the psychology so it was late afternoon when I got to my room. When I did, all I could see was a sea of plants all over my floor. All the guys in my wing had brought the plants I had in their windows down to my room and left them. No one wanted to be labeled from what the prof said. I spent the evening convincing each of the guys that I'd take full responsibility for their plants. They could simply say they were mine and cast all the blame onto me--just let me use their windows! By late evening I had all the plants back in their rightful spots. Whew, I was worried for a minute. Once again however, the statement of the professor made more permanent than ever my need to never tell my past.

In the spring I had the chance to try out for the two traveling quartets NNC sponsored. These singers were even paid for having fun all summer. By this time dad had sold the milk cows and had rented about 250 acres along with our own farm. He said I could come home and work on the farm for the summer with him and Ron. I thought this would be fine. I had made it a practice to come home fairly often through the school year to assist with harvest in the fall and some spring work needing done. Ron was now graduating from high school and was going to attend NNC also. This would be great I thought. I didn't try out for the quartets and went home. Besides, I had the quartet already and didn't want to conflict with it. We were all going our separate ways for the summer anyway intending to return to college and our singing the coming year.

As I got home I realized the fact that dad hadn't really changed. I'm not sure why I had thought he would, but it's something like childhood hope. Rich wasn't living at home now. He had moved into Homedale and was living with an aunt and uncle there. I recall one day when dad and I were headed out to do the morning irrigating. He asked me why I was so quiet? I asked what he meant by that? He said I had come home and had hardly said a word for three weeks. He was wondering if something was wrong? I remember thinking--something wrong? Is anything right? Why was I home? Why did I commit to coming back here? However, I was very much unable at that time to verbalize these feelings. In fact, most of what was inside me was deep-rooted confusion and hurt. I just made my mind up to be talkative when dad and I were together. This seemed to work for the rest of the summer.

Ron and I were able to get loans and grants for our college the coming year. Dad didn't have to be asked for any money and I know that was a good thing. We went off to college and for the most part our paths didn't cross very often. Sometimes we'd come home together. That year at Christmas, dad took all of us to California for our last trip there as a family. The trip to California at Christmas had been the highlight of almost every year growing up after we moved to Adrian. We'd get a neighbor to milk the cows and away we'd go for a week. Our relatives in California would take great care of us kids. We'd get extra presents from them--ones we didn't have to share with each other as most were at home. My oldest brothers and sisters would have us stay with them separate of dad and mom. This freed us to talk endlessly with them about "how things were with dad". All of them were sympathetic because they'd lived through it, too. I would take ample opportunity while we were there to do their dishes, help with laundry or whatever I could so they would hopefully keep me with them. My sis and my one aunt would tell me what good help I was. I'd even watch in the rearview mirror for a hundred miles or more when we'd be driving back thinking they'd pull up beside us. They'd tell dad they wanted me to stay with them instead of going back. This never happened and of course now, I understand why.

My sis Bonnie had moved to California and married Randy. They took us to Disneyland while we were there. That was so fun. We had been there a couple times with our Aunt Billie taking us. This time it was just us kids--Bonnie, Randy, Ron, Polly and me. They paid for everything. How fun that was.

My sophomore year in college introduced me to my first opportunity to work in a school. I had to put in a number of hours in an elementary school and then a high school. I started in the elementary. I was going to be a high school math teacher, but there was a magnet for me with those little kids in the elementary I couldn't explain. I went to my advisor on campus and talked with her. She said I could change my major to elementary education with a minor in math/science. That was perfect! I spent the rest of my 2.5 years in college catching up with the elementary ed classes, but I was able to graduate on time taking my last required courses the last term of my senior year. Remember, I had that draft number of 91 and my deferment from the army was only good for four years so I couldn't extend into a fifth. This shift to elementary ed was a life changer for me. I loved it and knew I'd found "heaven on earth". As I got into education I began to realize that it didn't matter where I taught, I loved any age. I just needed to have a chance to work with them.

The spring of my sophomore year our quartet did a spring tour. One of our members had relatives in the bay area of California so we arranged to sing at several churches there. Mike Benedick hadn't seen the ocean before so this was going to be exciting for him as we'd make a point to take a plunge into the Pacific even though it was only March. This trip brings up something I've never talked with anyone about but it is relevant to my recovery. It was on this trip that I had to sleep with another guy in a shared bed. We would have to do this for a number of nights, too. This was a huge step of faith for me. I laid awake long into the night hoping the one I slept with wouldn't try doing anything to me if I went to sleep. This anxiety eventually subsided, but it would return each trip, especially if I had to sleep with someone new.

At the end of my sophomore year Ron and I went back to the farm for the summer. Again, dad was renting the additional acres saying he'd give assistance to us. I had already done all the paperwork for our grants and loans so we were set with or without any assistance. I had the typewriter I'd been given so I routinely typed term papers for others which gave me needed spending money. I'd also sing for weddings, funerals and other events where often I was given a gratuity for doing so. I remember that Rich was also needing to move back home from our aunt and uncle's place. I don't recall why, but Rich had said he needed help. He told me he'd told dad he had a bed of his own which he didn't. In fact, he had nothing but a few clothes. He did have a pickup so he and I went to the used furniture store in Homedale where I paid for a used iron bed. It was either $20 or $25. We loaded it into the pickup and took it home. Mom was actually grateful to have the bed and this kept Rich from having yet another beating and verbal outburst from dad.

The summer came and went and Ron and I were back to NNC for his sophomore and my junior year. It was at Christmas time this year dad announced to us he would buy us a car so we could have a reliable way to get to and from home to college. It was now Christmas of 1970 and the car was a 1965 Chevy Impala. The best part for me was that it was blue with blue interior. It ran and that was good too! If memory serves me, the car cost $995.00. This was dad's one major contribution to Ron and me for our years of work for him. The year came and went and Ron and I were once again going home for the summer to work. This time Ron was not planning to return to college. He had completed two years and still didn't have a major so he decided to quit and work. He also had found "a love". Her name was Jann Paul. She was a keeper I had thought! His draft number was in the high 200's so he wasn't worried about being drafted into the war as I needed to be.

The summer of 1971 was not a good summer. Ron and I had moved our bedroom from the house to the milk barn. Dad had built a grade A dairy barn. My brother-in-law Sterling, Eunice's husband, drove out from Boise, Idaho each day to construct it. Dad had gotten a loan for this, but then he never used the barn. So, Ron and I put our bedroom in the front part of it. We thought getting further removed from dad was a good thing. For the most part it was. I was going to be going into my senior year and was starting the fall with student teaching at a new elementary in Boise, Valley View Elementary. I was going to need our car for the driving each day. Ron had agreed this was ok. He would drive dad's pickup since dad had talked him into working for him the coming year. Dad would treat him as a full partner in the farming and share all profits with him. Looking back, I don't know why we were such suckers. Each time, we believed, it would happen this time. Dad had also told me to not apply for any loans or grants. He wanted to pay for this last year for me. So, like Ron, I believed him and didn't apply for any financial assistance. There is a definition for insanity that I've learned in Celebrate Recovery that says: Insanity is doing the same thing over and over again, each time expecting different results. I was definitely caught in this with my hope of dad turning around his behavior.

As fall was approaching I told dad I would need the $700.00 for the first term's tuition, room and board. He said he didn't have the money and I'd need to find it elsewhere. I stood my ground and told him he couldn't do this to me. I had agreed to not apply for any assistance because of his promises and now it would be too late for any applications. I eventually won my case and dad borrowed the $700.00 from his bank in Homedale.

A bright spot for me as this year was beginning was that I had to do what was called a "September experience". This was for any student who was going to student teach. NNC didn't start early enough in the fall so the September experience gave one the opportunity to work with the beginning of a school year. Thus, one would work with their home school district to spend two weeks with a classroom teacher while they opened the year. My bright spot was that I was able to work these two weeks with the same 5th grade teacher who had inspired me to teach in the first place. As it turned out, this was going to be her retiring year. I was able to share with her all the inspiration she'd been to me and now I was just a year away from stepping into this career path. Mrs. Long was wonderful to be with. She had no idea her teaching had been this inspirational for me. At the end of the year she donated all her teaching boxes to me which I was able to put to good use for my start.

At the end of student teaching the fall of 1971, I went home for Christmas break. It was now time for paying 2nd quarter's tuition, thus I needed the next $700.00. Dad said I could talk all I wanted this time, but I'd be getting nothing from him. I didn't sleep that night from sheer worry and anger. I prayed and asked for God's intervention. The next day I called NNC to see what advice they had for me. The financial aid person told me they could likely give me a work study and to call my local bank. I called the bank in Homedale where dad did his banking. As only God would ordain, the bank had one student loan available for $1,000.00. With the work study I would need to work the other $400.00. Praise the Lord!

I was dating steadily a girl through the start of my senior year. One particular day she asked if she could use my car and I could hitch a ride with another student teacher at my same school in Boise. I arranged it so she could use the car. At supper that night while she and I were sitting with several friends she announced she'd made herself the key for the car like I'd told her she could do. She had said nothing to me ahead of time about doing this but I held my comments until we were walking back to her dorm following dinner. I asked her what she thought she was doing saying that when she knew good and well she'd said nothing to me about making this key. She tried to convince me I'd forgotten but I knew I'd not forget something as important as this. Besides, the car was half Ron's and for that reason alone I wouldn't give an extra key to someone. Later that night I called her and broke off our relationship. She had been the piano player for our quartet and twisting truth was something I'd encountered more than once with her.

My relationship with her began casually when she started playing for our quartet. She was a year younger than I and was an exceptionally good piano player. She could learn songs by ear, play sophisticated songs by reading notes and could also transpose quite easily from one key to the next. She was gifted. My roommate my junior year started dating her and by spring time they were quite serious. He had told me he was taking her to visit his parents right before spring break and there he was going to ask her to marry him. I was excited for them. Earlier that year I had prayed with him asking Jesus into his life and so I sure didn't want something interfering with this relationship.

Just two days before the weekend my roommate was taking her to his home, I was called by this girl--our piano player. She wanted to talk to me. We met after supper that night. She confided in me that she wasn't sure she was in love with my roommate. I told her she needed to let him know not revealing his intentions for the weekend. She went on to say she was in love with someone else. I asked if I knew him and she said, "Sort of." I asked who and she said it was me. I was stunned, shocked, complimented all at the same time. I told her this was not the right timing for this and she needed to come clean with my roommate and leave me out of the picture. That very night she broke up with my roommate and told him she was in love with me. I hadn't gone to my room until later that night, probably about 9:30 pm. When I entered it, it had been trashed like nothing I'd ever seen. Broken glass was everywhere. We had several coke glasses in the room. My roommate had taken all of them and thrown them against the walls, doors, closet doors and the glass was shattered all over the floor and into the wooden doors he'd hit. He was gone--all his clothes were removed, his desk was cleared and bedding was gone.

He had a married sister in town so I called her to see what had happened. She told me he'd called saying I'd betrayed him and he was moving home, quitting college. I was so sorry, yet, I was innocent of any wrong doing. I had tried to get the truth into the open, yet it didn't turn out that way at all. I had to talk to the dorm dad and show him the room. We did our best to remove the glass. They ended up replacing the closet doors. The glass in them was too embedded.

My roommate came back a week or so later to get the rest of his stuff. He came while I was in class. The sad part for me is I've never been able to talk to him again, even to this day. He did come back to NNC and graduate a year later. Over the years I've tried to contact him, writing him an apology letter, but all to no avail.

Later that spring, probably a month after my roommate left the scene, I asked this girl out. We would see one another because of her playing for us. I thought if she loved me I should try this out. For a few weeks everything seemed good. There were incidences where I'd question things said to me, but I'd always go back to the fact she loved me. As my senior year started and she lied to me about the car key, that was too much. Our relationship was through.

As the winter term of my senior year began and I had secured the finances to finish school, with the exception of the work study, I was on a downhill journey I thought. But as the weeks progressed, I found I was limited to the amount of time the college would let me work. I was in the kitchen washing dishes and they limited me to 10 hours a week. By the end of the winter quarter I had only earned enough to pay for my books and paying down $100 of $400 I owed. I was going into spring break and knew I needed a different job. I wouldn't get my diploma unless my debt was paid. There had been a new restaurant built close to the college so I walked down to it the morning of the last day of school prior to break. I had an hour between classes so I took advantage of this time. I asked if there were any openings and was told their night dishwasher had just quit that morning and could I start that night. I said, "YES!" The pastor and his wife where I'd been attending church during most of my time in college opened their home to me for the 10 days of break as the college shut down the dorms. I worked nine of the ten days almost 12 hours each day. When break was done I had the debt paid. I was overjoyed.

During the winter of this senior year I had begun to send out applications to surrounding school districts hoping to get an interview with one who wanted an upper elementary grade teacher. During the 10 days staying at my pastor's home I landed an interview. It wasn't one where I had applied. Mrs. E, the pastor's wife, had been substituting in Vallivue School District quite a lot. She had been teaching in West Canyon Elementary. It was a first year building, open-classrooms. The principal had shared with Mrs. E she was looking for teachers with experience in open classroom teaching and particularly men with that background. Mrs. E told the principal about me and so I was invited to come and meet with her. I wasn't sure if it was intended to be an interview or a talk. Either way I was excited and scared to death! After meeting with Mrs. Tucker, the principal, for about an hour she called the superintendent of the district and asked me to go meet with him. I drove from West Canyon to Vallivue High School where the superintendent's office was housed. I met with him for about 30 minutes and he had me sign a contract right then and there. Wow, talk about God helping me deal with my fears--I'd paid my college debt so I could graduate and at the same time I'd signed a teaching contract with the very district I'd hoped could be mine but never really dreamed it would be so. Yet, it happened. West Canyon was only a half mile from Deer Flat Church which would become my home church once I graduated and started my job.

A couple weeks into the spring term of my senior year I got a call from my ex-girlfriend. She was sorry she said about lying to me in the fall and wanted to know if we could get together again. To be honest with you, I was rather relieved. I was worried sick wondering what I was going to do going out into the world beyond college a single man. Most of the classmates were married or engaged by now and I was alone. I was actually living in a retired couple's home for the winter and early spring months. They had relatives in the East and had asked if I'd live in their home rent free to take care of things. This alone saved me a couple hundred dollars of dorm expense, so of course I was thrilled.

The secret of Rich's use of me left me thinking much of the time I must be like him or I wouldn't have been an attraction to him. The high school student who had wanted to have me involve myself with him also spurred on this thinking. Along with that, the comment the student had said in the dorm about my "backside" left me even more reinforced in this. Lastly, the professor who said what he did about guys who like plants were likely gay solidified my thinking. All this left me on red alert. I needed to have a girlfriend and eventually a wife so I "could look normal".

When my ex-girlfriend called me and asked if we could get together, I said that would be fine. For the reasons expressed above, I thought God must have brought this about to protect me just as he'd done helping me pay the debt and get a teaching job. We started getting together rather often after that. It was about 4-5 weeks later on a Sunday evening that we were talking about what life would be like as a married couple. In the midst of this she asked me a question that literally stopped me in my tracks. She said, "In this talking about marriage are you asking me or telling me?" The exact words were likely a little different, but this is the message I recall. I stuttered some and finally said, "I guess I am asking." She said that her answer was, "Yes." Just like that I was engaged! We called her parents and mine. Everything was now going to be OK!

From this point of becoming engaged until the wedding, many ducks seemed to lining up in a row. I was graduating with a degree in the very field I wanted to spend the rest of my life doing, I had already signed a contract with a district where I'd be working only a half mile from the church I'd soon be attending, and now, I was going to be normal because I'd be married. How much better could life get?

CHAPTER 8

The Months
before Marriage

My fiancé and I had set our wedding date to be August 17, 1972. It would take place in Tacoma, Washington where her parents were residing. It wasn't going to be an elaborate wedding since none of us had very much money. There will be more on this in a few paragraphs.

The retired couple for whose house I was caring returned mid-April of '72. I was needing to move at that time. I wasn't wanting to move back into the dorm so Mike Benedick and his wife Carol asked if I wanted to live the last few weeks with them. Mike was moving to California upon graduation trying to get into med school. He wanted to live there for a year to establish residency and work on his Masters at the time. The house was owned by Carol's brother and was a nice two bedroom house with a small yard and enough space for a "little garden". I could move in now and upon graduation, live there for the summer. Another friend, Terry, wanted to room with me during the summer. He was also engaged and would be working for the summer on the campus grounds. I had landed the restaurant job and they had asked me to be their night manager for the summer until I left for my teaching job.

During the last term of my senior year I was working at the restaurant from 3:00 pm until midnight. It was early May when I had walked from the restaurant to Mike and Carol's home where I now lived. When I walked into the living room Mike was watching TV with four other college friends. I tried to get into whatever movie was on but I was pooped and ready for bed. I was about to excuse myself when one of them said, "Shall we de-pants him or let him take his own off?" I said, "What!" They immediately pounced on me and began taking my clothes off. Mike tried to tell me it was a bachelor's party since I was now engaged! They stripped me down to my shorts, took me out onto the patio where they had a couple waste baskets full of water. They poured them over my head so I was soaking wet and loaded me in Mike's car. We drove to the shopping center on 12th Ave right where the restaurant is where I'd just come from. Stopping in the middle of the parking lot they pushed me out saying they'd see me back at the house. It was now about 12:30 am.

I quickly found a light pole and tried to blend into it. I waited until there were no cars coming in either direction and ran across 12th Ave which was a main road with 4 lanes. Once I got across it I found an E/W bound street that was partially lighted and headed up it. I thought when I got far enough east I could cut across to the street our house was on. To be honest, I had never been so scared in my life. The attack of these guys invaded every boundary I had, and believe me, I had lots of them when it came to touch and dress. They certainly didn't know this. It was fun and games for them.

I began to work my way up the street finding large bushes I could quickly run from one to the other. In less than an hour I was at the street so I could cut across the six or so blocks to our house. A car had come down the street I was on and I was desperately hiding. Once the car got beyond me I heard my name being yelled. It was Mike. He had returned to take me home but I was so scared I hadn't noticed the car's identification until he had passed. I was scared to yell myself for fear someone in a house would hear or see me. I was only in my underwear and what kind of a pervert would they think I am! I missed my ride. As I got to the street where I would head south I saw that two cars were coming from two different directions. I started to run to the bushes at the house to find this particular house had NO BUSHES! I ran to the corner of it and huddled into a tight ball hoping I'd blend into the bricks of the house. The two cars that were coming turned out to be cop cars. They stopped at the corner and began to talk to one another. All I remember is one of them pointed to the corner of the house where I was squatted down. The last thing I recall is taking off down the alley between houses running as fast as I could run. I was not only just in my underwear but I was also barefooted. To this day I can't tell you what happened and how far I ran. I finally came to my senses 30-40 minutes later. I was trudging through some yards in a new subdivision sinking to my calves in mud. I had dogs chasing me, barking away and porch lights were starting to come on. At the street corner was a wild rose bush. It had long draping branches so I crawled deep into it not even noticing the scratches from the thorns. I stayed there until the dogs left and the last porch light went off. I was totally lost (for me that doesn't take too much). I could see a lighted street a few blocks east of where I was so I took off to see what the street name was. By now I was fully conscious. My feet ached/ throbbed and my body was more than ready to find rest. I no longer cared if someone saw me close to being naked, I just wanted to get home. When I saw the street name I knew I had gone well past where I lived. I then walked the last 30 minutes on the sidewalk to get back home.

When I walked into the house I had been gone 2-3 hours. Mike was panicked. He had called the police after he'd gone looking for me and the two on the corner were there on purpose to take me home. How did I know they wanted to help me instead of arrest me for being so perverted? How would Mike know that this young man had a secret he could never reveal? Mike apologized and I went on to bed. It took a few days for my feet to feel comfortable in shoes again, but all this soon passed.

This was actually Mike's second time to "scare the pants off me". The first time wasn't quite so dramatic, but none the less, it was dramatic at the time. Our sophomore year our quartet was singing for a teen weekend in Twin Falls, Idaho. If you have been to Twin Falls you know there is a gigantic bridge over the Snake River canyon. It is over a thousand feet from the bridge to the water below. I am deathly afraid of heights and Mike knew this. He thought it would be funny to stop in the middle of the bridge as we were heading across. I instantly got out and started running across to get off the bridge. I have no recollection of the rest of this weekend. I don't even recall getting back into the car. My fears run deep within me but the nice thing is that so does my sense of humor. We laugh about all this now even though I could still kick him hard for this!

After my college graduation life took on a temporary calm. Terry and I lived in the house Mike and Carol vacated. We had our summer jobs, Terry working day shift and I worked from noon to midnight six days a week. Terry didn't cook nor did he clean. Our agreement was he would keep his bedroom door shut and I'd take care of the house. I had had enough experience cooking at home that I could do ok with this. On one occasion I had decided to make spaghetti. I knew it had hamburger in it and a sauce that was red. I went to the grocery store and bought the hamburger, spaghetti noodles, catsup and cheese. From having eaten my mom's spaghetti, I thought these ingredients looked like the right ones. I started with the noodles. I knew they had to be boiled. I put some in the boiling water but it looked like nothing at the time. I ended up putting all the noodles in and then needing to change the pot three times, each time getting a bigger one. I cooked the hamburger and mixed it with the noodles. I thought somehow that would help break up those ones that were so stuck together. I then dumped in a bottle of catsup for the red sauce. It seemed redder than mom's so I thought that must be where the cheese came in to play. I cut the cheese into smaller pieces and dumped them into the mix stirring it until it was all melted. By now I had a huge pot of what no one else would call spaghetti. I left it on the stove for Terry's lunch and I left for work. When I got home that night I thought I'd find it in the trash. Instead, Terry was still up waiting to thank me for the delicious meal. He'd had his fiancé over that day for lunch and they thought it was so good she came back that night for supper with it again. I was relieved and they were thankful! A great ending to what I thought would be a tragedy.

Because I had taken over the rent payments for the house in June, I had to hurry to get my garden established. I spaded a strip along the carport where I planted beans and tomatoes and then spaded a spot in the corner of the front lawn for flowers. In the backyard I spaded another area for the remaining garden. The thing that amazed me was when I was told to be careful spading up lawn. The next renter may only wish to have lawn rather than a garden. I thought--"What? Someone would rather have lawn than garden? How sad is that!" As sad as this seemed to me, I've found the statement to be much truer than I've ever dreamed. Only a small portion of our world truly likes to garden--at least to the degree I do.

The summer of '72 brought a shocking letter to me. I received a letter from the draft board in Salem, Oregon. I was registered in Oregon and so my accountability went back to them. I was to report for a physical the day after I was returning from my honeymoon and a day before I was to report to work at my first teaching job. That year the draft was taking all men with a draft number of 125 or under. Mine was 91 so I had to report. I'll tell more about this in a few paragraphs.

As the summer rolled into August it was time for me to plan the trip to Tacoma for our wedding. The workers at the restaurant threw a shower for me. It was so thoughtful. Being a guy I had never participated in a shower before. They told me I deserved it and since the wedding was in Washington, they would be unable to attend. I was really touched. One of the guys I worked with was going to be in the wedding so on my last day he drove through the night with me so we could get to Tacoma without falling asleep. He rode back with one of the other wedding attendants who came from Nampa.

CHAPTER 9

Married Life

The wedding itself is somewhat of a blur for me. I was experiencing so much trauma about what a groom does on his wedding night that I could think about little else. I use the word trauma because I felt trauma rather than excitement. I only knew sex through the lens of abuse--what was it like in real life?

It was 2:00 am when we finally arrived at our hotel where we were to spend our first night. We hadn't eaten since lunch the previous day so we first went to the hotel restaurant and had a dinner. I couldn't talk much due to my intense fears. My new wife seemed happy and didn't need me talking much anyway. We were soon in our room and in bed with one another. It was at this point I literally broke into sobs. I confessed to her I was "virgin" (which wasn't a new revelation to her) but I also confessed--I didn't know what I was to do. She gently guided me and "OH MY WORD--WASN'T THAT A GREAT MOMENT!" I knew then things would be fine.

The remainder of our honeymoon went well. We had made plans to go to Canada which was fun and exciting. As we got back to my wife's parents to load unwrapped wedding gifts and pack for our move to Nampa, my wife's dad told her he would not be able to pay for her last year of college. We had absolutely no financial means for doing this. My gross salary was going to be $500.00/month as a starting teacher. We had a rent payment of $80.00 and a car payment of $75.00. This would be half of my take home pay before utilities and groceries. In nine months I would have to start paying back school loans too as well as pay back the ones my wife had forthcoming. My wife and I decided she would work the coming year and maybe she could finish the following one. Her dad suddenly changed his mind and said he would pay. By that time we felt it best to keep our plan in place. My wife wasn't sure we wanted to be dependent on this promise.

We left the next day to drive from Tacoma to Nampa. We loaded our little Datsun sedan and a U-haul carrier for its top with our treasured gifts and my wife's clothes. Our apartment we had rented was furnished so we didn't need any furniture. The day following our arrival in Nampa I had to report to Ontario, Oregon for my army physical. As I was going through the line of duties I asked one officer what I'd need to do if I were a conscientious objector. I was quickly told if I were a CO, I would have already applied for it. I told him I hadn't killed anyone and wasn't sure I could, but that didn't seem to help.

The following day was my first day at West Canyon Elementary School where I would be teaching 5th grade in a team of three but in a "pod" with three 6th grade classes along with our three 5th grade ones. Also, in the center of the pod was a special education class for the 5th and 6th grade kids. I had to report to my principal that I'd just had my army physical the day before and I was fearful I may be enlisted. She didn't seem alarmed, but I was.

School soon began for the students and I had my first class. I had 31 students in my homeroom. My team and I had determined that since I had been a math major and neither one of them liked math as much as reading, I would take the struggling math students. This was our thinking--the teacher's strength could off-set the students' struggle. I, in turn, took the highest reading students for that block since I had the least amount of college preparation in the field of language arts. I had always had good grades in Reading/English but that was from a student's standpoint, not a teaching one. Fortunate for me, I had student taught in a scenario similar to this so I had background given to me by my supervising teacher. Mrs. Long, my past 5th grade teacher had by this time retired from Adrian Elementary and I had taken her boxes of materials to my room where I actually had things on my bulletin boards!

By mid-September I had received my induction papers for the army. My date to report to duty was something like Oct. 21, 1972. I had told my pastor about this and he said he would be praying God would find a way out of this for me. I didn't tell him why I was so fearful of going, but he seemed very concerned for me. Little did I know the steps Mrs. Tucker, my principal, was taking. Just two days before my induction date Mrs. Tucker walked into my classroom with a letter. She showed it to me and much to my surprise, it was a letter from the general in charge of the draft from Salem, OR. It was granting me a postponement to my induction until January 15, 1973. She had told him that West Canyon was a new school built to support team teaching in an open setting. I had been hired because I had specific training meeting these needs and teachers with this background were next to impossible to find in Idaho. I thanked both God and Mrs. Tucker! On January 10, 1973 Mrs. Tucker got a 2nd letter granting me an extension to my delay until June 15, 1973. This way I could finish my contracted year. That June was when President Nixon abolished the draft. This took place on June 1st. The Vietnam War was ending, the draft was abolished and I didn't have to report to duty. The relief this gave me is impossible to put into words.

This autobiography isn't to be centered on my marital sex life, but I do need to step into it a little in order to explain the impact the sexual abuse had on me. As my wife and I progressed in our marriage, sex was something I never talked about. In my adolescent years I could never ask any questions for fear someone would want to know why I was asking and I'd have to talk about my abuse. Now I was married and deathly afraid to talk with my wife about our sex. Luckily for me, she opened the door for conversations and to broaden my learning in this sensitive topic. It didn't matter that I truly enjoyed every moment, I also deeply struggled blocking out the mental images of Rich. I kept thinking this would fade in time and I'd end up being normal like everyone else. This was a sad hope that never came to fruition. If sex had been our only problem we may have been able to overcome it. New ones began to appear as our marriage progressed.

Our first winter was 1973. We were asked by Representative Symms, later Senator Symms, if we'd want to live in their home which was much closer to my school and our church. We were living in Nampa and I was driving 15 miles each way to commute. Rep. Symms had just been elected for his first term in office. They were not sure what they wanted to do with their home at the time so we were asked to live in it for a period of time. I had their oldest son in my class that year and they also went to the same church we attended. This was another Godsend for us. We didn't have to pay rent any longer and they were also going to pay most of the utilities. This gave us a chance to pay school loans to a greater degree. Also, my wife had been in a car accident earlier that fall leaving our car totaled. We had insurance, but certainly not enough to replace the car with a reliable one. This cost savings gave us enough to save a down payment.

These were a couple of wonderful years. My wife and I were able to save money and get college loans paid down. We began to buy some appliances that we found and could use when we had our own place. A puzzling thing to me was my wife's lack of sharing thoughts. I would ask for her thoughts and rarely would I get them. Mostly what I got were statements of compliance. I knew she had thoughts but I couldn't seem to motivate her to share them. I recall telling her once that I felt we had a dark veil between us. I could never get to the other side of it and actually didn't as long as we were married.

After our first year at this home I had an unexpected visitor one evening. There was a knock at our door and looking out the window I saw that it was my brother Rich. He drove an orange pickup. I didn't know he even knew where we lived. It was in early spring so I went outside and welcomed him. He told me he had come to talk. He was living again with my aunt and uncle in Homedale. He had recently attended a revival service in Parma with them. He had gone to the altar and prayed. He had asked for healing from his homosexuality and God had granted it to him. He was now at my home asking me for my forgiveness for the years of abuse he had done to me.

He wanted to take both my hands which I let him do. He said he wanted to know that what I said to him was confirmed by my spirit that he could feel from holding my hands. I stood there and assured him I held no resentment towards him. I was happy for him that he'd found peace from this torment he had struggled with all his life. He said that he felt the truth of what I told him in my spirit. With that, he left. When I re-entered our home my wife asked me what that was about. I simply told her that Rich had come by to apologize for some past things in our growing up.

We were able to live in Symms' home for two years. During the second year we qualified for a subsidized housing loan and built our first house. It was there we had our first child—Amy Joy. I really thought we were doing great now. I was 25 and was loving my work. My wife had been working in a bank and was now quitting after Amy was born the end of August, 1975.

It was in the school year of 1975-76 that God opened a door for me that has helped shape my life and career from that point forward. Mrs. Tucker, my principal, asked me to talk with her one day in her office. She informed me her husband, Dr. Ward Tucker, was the Dean of Education at the College of Idaho in Caldwell. They offered a Masters in Education Administration and I should look into it. She went on to say that she wouldn't be principal here at West Canyon forever. I thanked her for the information but walked out wondering how she thought something like this graduate program could ever be paid for on my limited salary?

Within the week of Mrs. Tucker talking to me I was approached by one of the people at school telling me her husband had some money invested that wasn't earning them any interest. If I were interested in going back to school they would be willing to fund it for me and charge me only the additional interest they were making at the time. The third thing that happened was the secretary of the school called me in and said her husband was the manager of a men's clothing store in Caldwell. They were wanting an extra hand sometimes on weekends for the store as well as full time during the summer. If I were interested, I should go talk to Orville, her husband. These were all disconnected conversations but extremely well connected in God's timing.

I did all three of them and the summer of 1975 I started my Master's program at College of Idaho, began working at Nafziger's Mens' Store in Caldwell and took my first loan from these dear friends. As only God would ordain, as each semester ended during these two years of graduate studies, I had worked enough at Nafziger's to pay back what I had borrowed. In the Fall of 1977 I graduated with my degree and it was all paid.

It was in the winter of '76 a first crisis hit in our marriage. I won't go into it as it isn't just my story to tell. However, after this crisis and a similar one a couple months later, we ended needing to sell our home. The last three years of our marriage we lived in a rental, farm house which at least kept me in the country—a strong need for me. Our 2nd child was born in April, 1977, Amber Jean.

The summer before we moved to the rental farm house another tragedy hit. It was in the evening that our phone rang. In answering it I was being told that my brother Rich had drowned in the Snake River. It was the latter part of July and grain harvest. He'd been working with a couple other young men on a grain harvest crew over by Wilder. The three had driven back to Homedale together. On the way they decided to hit a swimming hole at the river to wash off the harvest dust.

Rich was no swimmer and hadn't gone out very far into the water. However, there was a drain ditch next to the swimming hole and its water had deepened the spot Rich dog-paddled into. He apparently tried to stand up to find no bottom. He quickly began to panic and scream. The other two were swimming out into the river and turned to help. One went for additional help while the other tried to rescue Rich getting him to shore. Rich was little but strong and almost drowned the helper in his attempts. He finally broke away from Rich's grasps. Rich went down at that point never to resurface.

It was the next afternoon before they found his body in the murky water. My dad and two brothers were at the river when they brought his body to land. I hadn't gone. I couldn't bring myself to this scene. I couldn't put perspective to all of it. Rich had apologized to me and was now forgiven. Why this?

His funeral was set and I was asked to sing a couple songs for it. I was a wreck before and after each song but made it through them. My wife played for me. She just thought I felt bad because he was my brother.

After the funeral all of my siblings and spouses gathered at mom and dads for a family dinner. Everyone had come for the funeral and we wanted to take advantage of everyone being present. We were mostly done with dinner when I couldn't stand being with the crowd any longer. Dad and mom at the time had retired from the farm moving closer to Caldwell. They had rented a little farm house well into the country. This allowed me to take off on foot as I had done so many times on our farm while I was growing up. When I got far enough away from their house I began to sob and scream. I yelled at God asking him why he'd take Rich to heaven and leave me here with this continuous torment? What was I to do now? No one knew and no one could ever know. I would be branded for life if the word ever leaked out. I stayed out for an hour or more and finally returned. By then I was able to address the family. I wasn't questioned about leaving. Everyone needed to process their grief in their own way. I was probably just needing to process mine, they likely thought.

CHAPTER 10

Divorced Years

In 1979 I took a small trip with my pastor attending a conference he was wanting me to be part of. I at this time was leading our church's worship as well as heading much of the Christian education work. Pastor Jim asked me how my marriage was doing. He was aware of some tough times we'd experienced previously. I told him I thought we were doing better than we had in a long time. Within a month however, I found out that my marriage was on the rocks and I was headed for a divorce. It was the end of July in 1979 that my wife told me she didn't love me any longer and wanted the divorce. I knew money was an issue for us. I had just been hired to be the new principal at my school, West Canyon replacing Mrs. Tucker, retiring principal. This would increase my salary by a third, yet none of this mattered.

We tried different ways to work through some changes thinking it might allow us to repair damages in the marriage. My wife moved out for a few days but returned telling me she wouldn't do this. I thought maybe if I moved out giving her space she would work through the emotional troubles. Everyone has marital problems, right? I'll never forget the moment of telling Amy and Amber I was moving out. Amy was 4 and Amber was 2. Amy was old enough to understand the fact I would be gone. Her response shocked me. She said, "Daddy, who is going to take care of you if you don't live with us?" I assured her my sis, Eunice would do this since I was going to live temporarily with her and her husband, Sterling. I realized what a caring little girl I had.

This temporary move turned into a permanent one. By early October, '79, the divorce was final. My wife had gone to a mutual, lawyer friend who had worked out an agreement for visitation with the girls spending half their time with me and half with their mom. The day of the divorce I found out that while the divorce was being decreed by the judge my ex-wife was having everything in the house loaded onto a truck and when she got home from the courthouse, she left for Tacoma, Washington along with our two daughters. I was told this by the person who was her witness at the courthouse. I think my ex-wife may have asked her to let me know. All of a sudden my kids were 500 miles away and I didn't even have an address or phone number for them. The visitation we had worked through was meaningless.

Even though I felt like a victim in much of this, I also knew "I had it coming." My ex-wife had married someone very tarnished who kept it all a secret. I knew I wasn't worthy of being a dad to my girls. I knew God must have taken them 500 miles away so they'd be safe. Who was to say I wouldn't end up just like Rich and have a terrible parenting problem just like my dad. They would be the victims of all this just as I had been. By this time I'd heard and read that abused people abuse. This would be me so God was protecting my kids and now ex-wife (or so I thought).

When I had moved out to give my wife space prior to the divorce, as I mentioned, I moved in with my oldest sister and her husband. Eunice was enough older than I that her kids were all grown and they had just built a new home in the country west of Caldwell—most convenient for my driving. They had extra room and said it would be fine. Little did they or I know it would last a year. For me, it was a haven. Eunice became my best counselor and friend. Even though we were siblings and sometimes spat with one another as such, she endlessly listened to me, gave me sage advice and fed me great meals. She even did the ironing of my shirts! I really didn't have the resources to rent another place. Unbeknownst to me until my ex-wife had moved, she had several debts left unpaid also in my name. The savings each of our little kids had in the bank were also gone. The money had been withdrawn and I had no idea what it had been used for. Sterling, my brother-in-law, and Eunice told me I could earn my keep and save the rent money to pay these debts. I did just that. They burned wood in their fireplace for heat and the fireplace was a wood "hog". That fall I split 14 cords of wood and helped cut most of it on weekends where we'd take Sterling's truck to the mountains. I told Sterling that firewood was the only heat that warmed you three times: once when cutting it, another when splitting it and lastly when you burned it.

During the first six months after the divorce I cried myself to sleep nightly. If I had been alone I think I would have ended it all. My only respite was going to work and getting so consumed at school I could think of nothing else. This would take care of the daytime hours. That was why it was so nice to have Eunice and Sterling when I got "home". Eunice was a homebody so I could count on her always being there at the end of the day.

The other support I had was the previous pastor of Deer Flat and his wife. Jim and Lois had left their positions as senior pastor and wife of the church earlier in 1979. Jim hadn't taken another church at the time and was working temporarily in a secular field. Their kids were grown so their nights weren't as full as they had been with their church work and rearing their children. I would often go to their house when I was needing spiritual guidance or just another ear other than Eunice's. Jim had a great sense of humor so he was almost always able to bring some cheer into my life. He and Lois were wonderful listeners and friends. They knew my ex-wife and me almost better than any other couple. They also understood the hurt I was going through and cast no judgment on me like so many others in our church had done. I really felt safe being with them. It was truly Jim's spiritual guidance that helped me eventually move on with my life. An example of this was a year after the divorce my ex told me she was sorry we had divorced and thought we should remarry. I felt like I had to do this so I could reunite with my kids. In talking with Jim about this he gave me very sound advice. He first asked if my ex-wife had changed from the person she was when she divorced me? I knew she hadn't. She was wanting to separate from her husband now and wanted me to fill the gap. Jim went on to say that my girls needed someone they could grow up knowing was stable. If I fell back into my ex's instability I would likely appear to them just as unstable as they would see her. This has proven to be very true as they grew into their adult years. I'm most grateful for that wonderful man Jim and his wife Lois.

There was one other tribute I'd like to make to Jim. Early in my married life on a Sunday night, Pastor Jim challenged the congregation to commit to daily Bible reading for one year. We were to sign a pledge card only if we were willing to make this commitment and live up to it. I was most willing and desirous of this spiritual step. Little did I know how much I would need this discipline in my life as I grew older. That year was grueling. Some days I'd only get two to three minutes of reading done--a verse or two. However, I stuck to my commitment of Bible reading for the year. This discipline has stayed with me from then to today. What used to be a few minutes is now routinely an hour. It has become much more personal today with learning to journal along with the daily devotional time and Bible reading. However, as these steps developed, I already had the daily discipline well established.

After my divorce I began to be bombarded with visitors from our church who wanted to know what had happened and how they could help. Some of them were sincere in their wishes to help. Some were more focused on how I needed to straighten out my life--after all, I had just run off this precious soul who had been our church pianist along with our two cute little girls. They had been told things that weren't true, yet I didn't ever want to be the one who told the truth. The truth would seem to place blame on my ex-wife when the deeper truth was that she, without knowing, had saved our kids from ruin and she deserved a much better husband than I could ever be. I simply quit going to church for about six months. I did try a couple times to slip in the back door and into the sanctuary after the service had begun. This set me into a spiraling mess. As I walked in the back I could hear the children in the kid's department. I ran to get away from this as it reminded me of my own two who had been part of this group. As I got into the sanctuary the congregation was singing and the music scorched my soul so deeply I just ran out and didn't return for many months. No one could know the depth of despair I felt during this time. The longing to have my children back, to be part of the church I loved serving the God I had wanted to please.

Shortly after I had returned, I was given an envelope by a lovely, little, older lady in our church by the name of Dovie. She was probably in her 80's at this time. She and I had known one another for 10 years. She'd always bring the same sack of candy to church each week to give to people. I called them her "Dovie mints". They were those pink candies that to me tasted like Pepto-Bismol. I loved the taste so they were always a treat for me. Little had I known that in Dovie's early years, she had been divorced. Her letter became something I would read daily if not several times a day. In it she told me I must be loved dearly by God. He would never allow someone to be hurt as severely as I had unless he knew they could endure and use it for good in their lives. At the time, these were the kindest words anyone had said to me. I use to tell God that I knew she was way off base, but I was sure thankful someone believed in me.

During this time in my life, money was in short supply and I had many bills to pay, many of them left for me to address. Even though I was a principal now, the school district had discovered a huge debt they had to pay. A consequence for me was that I was only paid a salary which was .5 of an administrative one. Thus, my salary was not much larger than it was when I was teaching. This step was corrected the following year, but it made my financial recovery very heavy the first year. I had always been one who tithed on my gross income thinking that was the right thing to do. After so many disappointing realities in my life, I told God I was going to cut back on my giving and only give to Him the tithe on my net income. I still loved Him but He just hadn't taken care of me in spite of my best efforts to be a good man for Him. How confused I was at this time. Little did I know about the depth of this confusion both about God, giving to Him and the difference between giving to Him and surrendering to Him. I address this deeply in Part III.

Since Eunice and Sterling's home was new, the yard was only partially landscaped. Sterling was working full time in Boise as a building contractor and had little time to spend in the yard. He told me he would pay for whatever improvements I wanted to make with it--that was like giving a blank check to a boy in a toy store! They already had a nice garden spot so Eunice and I spent much time with the vegetables grown in it. But my fun was with all the flower gardens and roses I saw in my head that could now be made real in the yard. I made endless trips to the nurseries in the area always getting Sterling's approval even though he kept saying it was all fine with him. These were all moments of bliss for me. I had never expected my tragedy to have moments of happiness in it.

There were a couple of, not so blissful moments too! One Saturday I was helping Sterling with a construction project he was doing in the yard. He needed an extension cord that was run to the house. I disconnected it and brought it to him not realizing what the cord was taking power to. About a week later Eunice informed Sterling and me that the freezer upstairs in the house had gone bad and all the frozen chickens (50 or more) she had bought were now thawed and spoiled. She had dumped them all that day. Sterling and I quickly went to investigate to find the power cord I had disconnected the week prior was the one feeding the freezer. The upstairs of their home was unfinished at this time so Sterling had brought power to these few items through this power cord. I felt terrible! They didn't seem to blame me, but I sure did!

The months with Eunice and Sterling brought much healing for me. The work needing to be done was like salve to an open wound. I needed the hard labor to work out the intense emotional upheaval I had buried. In the fall of 1980 I had found a little house up for rent and only a mile from West Canyon. I secured it and made my departure to life on my own. The teachers at school gave me a surprise house warming that same fall. It was a Friday afternoon, the kids had all boarded their buses and I had twenty to thirty boxes of school supplies to get into the supply rooms of the school. In those days we had almost no custodial help or aide help so much of this I did. As I took a hand truck full of supplies through the first and second grade wing I saw two 8' tables laden with gifts. I quietly went through the area to get to the storage room when I heard, "Earnie, come over here, this is for you!" I ignored them at first thinking they were teasing me. They assured me they weren't and I was welcomed to one of the most thoughtful moments I've ever encountered in my life. This staff had rallied between themselves and my sis Eunice to literally round up everything I needed to start life in this new little rental. I had furniture, kitchen appliances, sheets and towels, dishes, canned food, fresh baked bread and so much more. I weep now writing this. Little did I know how much people cared for this broken man. I was supposed to be their boss but God was using them to be His hands in showing me how much He and they cared.

In the fall of '80 after moving into the house I had returned to Deer Flat thinking I needed to turn over this new leaf. The summer prior to I had received a postcard in the mail inviting me to a single's party being held at Lake Lowell's lower dam. I instantly threw it away wondering why I was getting something in the mail for a "single". Almost before I could take a second breath my thinking was checked. I suddenly realized I AM a single. I wasn't ready to attend anything like this, but I needed to address my own thinking. One of our associate pastors at church had asked me to think about starting a singles' ministry at Deer Flat. I told him I would consider it knowing I'd never do it. When this card came in the mail and God awakened me to my new reality, I went back to Steve, the associate, and said I would do this but I couldn't do it alone. He put me in touch with Dick and Vonnie who had said they could help a ministry like this, but couldn't find the time to lead it. I knew them well having sung for their wedding eight or nine years prior to this.

As I settled into my little house I also began hosting a Tuesday night singles' Bible study there. We started with six or seven and within the year it grew to over 20. This was a newer type ministry in our area so as the word got out, singles from other churches began to check us out. As the singles in our group began to bond, we felt the need to promote socials as well as our Bible study. Different ones would take responsibilities to promote and structure these. They turned into some of my funniest memories.

It was now 18 months since my divorce and I had begun to date a lady in our singles' group. Our first date was something else for me! I have always been directionally impaired. She lived in Parma and I was going to her house. I don't even recall what we were to do that night. All I recall are the directions she'd given me to her house and "how easy it was to find it"! I got to Parma an hour ahead of time. Somewhere before entering town coming from the east on Hwy 20, there was to be a right turn onto a truck route bypassing main street. I was to take the truck route as her house was one block off it. Well, for 45 minutes I drove slowly into town over and over again trying to find this truck route's right turn. Finally in desperation, I drove back out of town and began driving into town in the borrow pit. I knew no turn could happen without it impacting the borrow pit. Well, I found it! I know now just how panic disrupts sound thinking and I was into panic that night! I found the house and even had one minute to spare. She and I seemed to hit it off and months later we got engaged. We had set a date for marriage the following June so the school year would be over. About three weeks ahead of the wedding she told me she just couldn't follow through with this. Her two children were from two different men. If she were to marry again, it needed to be with the father of one of her kids. Somehow I respected that, but mostly I chalked this up to God's protecting her and her boys as He did my ex-wife and my girls. I just wasn't worthy of marriage.

I remember driving from the house of my now unengaged lady friend to Eunice's place. I needed someone to talk to. I told her I didn't feel like I was worthy of this gal and Eunice tried to tell me I was off base in this thinking. She then asked me how I was doing with God in all this. My response even shocked me--I said, "If I knew where God's butt was, I'd kick it!" I didn't go on to say anymore, but deep inside I couldn't figure out why God was doing so much to protect everyone else and I was being left carrying the baggage and hurt.

Within a couple weeks I drove to Washington to get my girls and have them with me for a month in the summer. These were most precious times for me. I would relish the days and moments within the days. I had moved by now into an older farmhouse on the land of some good friends in our church. They had experienced some poor renters and hoped I'd consider living there. When I saw the house I couldn't believe it. It was like an old cottage. It had a cute yard and some landscaping and a large place for a garden. The fact it hadn't been nurtured for years didn't matter. My love for gardening and landscaping could overcome any yard's demise. It was well off any main road so I could be as hidden as I needed. The girls and I had a wonderful couple summers there.

CHAPTER 11

Kathy

Having experienced my second rejection I had told myself I was to move on with life as a single. God didn't want me to be married and I would somehow be ok with that. One of the teachers at my school had something else in mind for me, at least her husband did and she was being his "mouthpiece". During the school year she kept telling me about Kathy Wolfe. This teacher and her husband had property in Wallowa County, Oregon and would spend ample time there in the summers and on weekends. They would invite me to go with them to meet Kathy but I wasn't about to put myself through another relationship to be hurt again. These invitations and messages kept happening throughout the school year.

One spring, Friday afternoon, Charlene, the teacher, came into my office saying, "You can't fire me for this, because it's all Chuck's fault. The Kathy I've been telling you about is at our house for the weekend. She came thinking she has a blind date with you. Chuck told her it was all arranged. You need to come to our house tomorrow night and six of us will all go out to dinner together. You won't have to be alone and in a few hours it will all be over."

I could hardly speak! "You did what?" I said.

She assured me of the message, "I wouldn't have to be alone and it would end quickly." She told me the time and I reluctantly said I'd be there.

I can't begin to tell you how many bouts of diarrhea I experienced that Saturday before going to their home. When I arrived I was greeted nicely by Charlene. Kathy wasn't quite ready and so hadn't come to the living room yet. I was introduced to the other couple who had brought Kathy with them from Wallowa. They, with Chuck and Charlene would make the six going out together. In a few minutes Kathy began to descend the stairs of Chuck and Charlene's home. This is literally the way it happened--I first saw these feet and then legs. I then saw more of the body descending and finally I saw her face. She wasn't just pretty, she was glowing. She had pretty blondish hair and seemed so eloquent. We were introduced and within a few minutes it dawned on Chuck that none of us had a vehicle which would accommodate six adults. In spite of my previous behavior I had been stricken! I told him that wasn't any problem, Kathy could ride with me in my little pickup and we'd follow them. Knowing how insistent I'd been about not being alone or even going on this date, they told me they could drive two cars. However, I, being stricken, assured them I wanted to drive. Actually, I wanted time to get to know this lovely lady.

We were going to drive to Boise for dinner which would be a 45 minute drive. I knew Kathy had never married and so I was driven to let her know right off the bat that I was anything but pure and clean. I told her about my first marriage, my kids, my divorce, my 2nd attempt getting engaged and that didn't work. I wanted her to know she was simply too good for this guy. I couldn't get past the fact that she seemed ok with all this information. I thought, "doesn't she get it? I'm not her type! I'm tarnished with a capital T!"

After dinner and we were going to go back to Chuck and Charlene's, I suggested that Kathy and I go our separate way and hit the movie theatre where Chariots of Fire was showing. I'd just seen it the weekend before and Kathy hadn't seen it yet. We went and afterwards I took her back to Wikstrom's home. She and the other couple were leaving the next morning to head back to Wallowa.

Sunday morning came and I was at church warming up with our choir. I was standing next to a friend who sang tenor with me. All of a sudden across the back of the sanctuary walked Kathy Wolfe. I instantly dropped the choir music I was holding. My friend asked what was wrong and I said nothing. He informed me I was now holding the music he was trying to read upside down! I just said I was having a bad morning. The choir sang for both services and this was the first one. After it I usually attended a Sunday School class but Kathy was now sitting in first service and on top of that, she was sitting right in front of Eunice, my sis and another relative of mine. I was in the choir room trying to decide what to do when a friend saw me and asked what was wrong. I told her my dilemma and she simply asked, "What do you want to do?" What a simple question to a tremendous problem! I said I wanted to go sit by her and she said, "Then do it!"

As I got to the sanctuary Kathy was sitting in the middle of a pew for which I had to stumble over four bodies in order to sit by her. I did this and never said a word to her or anyone else. At the end of the service she thanked me for the evening we had the night before. I said something like I had enjoyed it too. In all honesty, I don't know what I said--I was way too nervous. She asked if it would be ok to write and I said that would be fine. She asked for my address and I gave it to her. She then said good-bye and walked out.

When I got home after church I suddenly realized I had given her my information but had gotten nothing from her. I was wanting to thank her for coming and to tell her how much I did enjoy our time together. The next day at school I asked Charlene for Kathy's address. I was then able to get a thank you card and mail it to her.

The following week Charlene informed me she, Chuck and their two kids were going to Wallowa. They were staying with the friends who had come bringing Kathy the week before. I was invited to go with them. This time I was excited, and yet still very nervous. We drove there on a Friday evening. Kathy and I spent the entire Saturday together. I had never been to Wallowa, Oregon. She told me some people called it the Swiss Alps of America. I could quickly see why even though at that point in time I'd never seen the Swiss Alps. Her family had a large cattle ranching business there. Kathy had been living and working in San Francisco area but had come home for a few weeks taking a break from work and having finished her MBA at Berkeley. Her dad had offered her a chance to stay and work for them and she took him up on his offer. Chuck had told me she was a ranching girl so I had envisioned a girl in cowboy boots who could lasso a steer and wrestle him to the ground, brand him and shoo him away while she was lassoing the next one. I was quickly to learn that even though she was raised on the ranch where all this took place, she was never involved in any of it nor wanted to be. She loved the country, but the girl I'd fantasized and feared was not the one sitting next to me.

In the weeks ahead Kathy and I made numerous trips to see one another. The school year had ended and I was wrapping up my work preparing for the summer where I would soon go to Washington to bring the girls to Idaho for the coming six weeks. Kathy had asked me how she'd meet them. I had told her I didn't know meaning that I didn't know. That was all. I hadn't really thought about it yet and that's all I meant. She thought it meant I didn't intend for her to meet them.

My birthday being July 1, Kathy had invited me to come to Wallowa for my birthday and she'd fix me a birthday dinner. We were then going to go to a children's camp her church was having and do the music for them. The night before I was to leave for this trip my sis Eunice had me over for a birthday dinner. She had invited a few of our family and it was a nice evening. After everyone had gone she said she wanted to talk to me. It was getting close to 10:00 pm so I was eager to get home and to bed so I'd be rested for the drive to Wallowa the next morning. She started our conversation saying how nice she thought Wallowa would be in the fall. Not having a clue what she was meaning, I said, "Yeah, I'm sure it is." She then said, "Think about it, the trees would be so beautiful with all their colors." I said yes, I could see that. She then said, "Well, what do you think?" I asked, "Think about what?" She then went straight to her point saying, "Listen little brother, if you let this gal slip through your fingers, it will be the dumbest thing you have ever done!" I told her I thought so too. Then she pulled out the bull's-eye and said, "I'm talking about you asking her to marry you when you go up tomorrow."

Now little brother got it! I said I just couldn't do that. I had not even told her I loved her. I knew she didn't know just how tarnished I really was. She knew nothing about Rich and me, but no one did at this point. I left saying this just wouldn't happen. Her parting words to me were, "Go home and pray about this. God would make it clear I was to propose. I just needed to listen to Him." She also told me to come back by the next morning on my way to the freeway so I could tell her what my plan was. As I got home that night I was so perplexed that sleep wasn't going to happen. I called my good friend Scott who lived in Boise. I told him what Eunice had just said. He gave me a man's perspective. He asked, "Do you think you will drive to Wallowa in the winter months on the snow and ice?" I assured him I didn't want to do this. He then said, "Do you want to sleep through another winter being alone on those cold nights?" I assured him I didn't want that either. His next response, "Then ask her to marry you and have the wedding in the fall like Eunice is telling you."

I finally went to bed thinking God had spoken through the two of them and I went to sleep. Fitfully through the night I kept awakening and with each time growing less and less confident. When I drove to Eunice's that morning I told her I would not be asking her to marry me. I just wasn't meant to be married anymore. She let me know she disagreed with me but my resolve was firm.

The drive to Wallowa from Caldwell is about four hours. I had lots of time to process with God as I drove that July 1st. I had turned 32 years old that day. It was about 11:30 am when I pulled into the parking lot of Kathy's folks' ranch office. She was waiting for my arrival and upon seeing my pickup pull in, exited the building. We weren't staying at the ranch. Kathy had been living in her folks' vacation home on Wallowa Lake. So, she got in her car and I, driving my pickup, followed her. This is another 30 minute drive. When Kathy had walked out of the office I saw her sparkly face. I knew I didn't want to let her slip through my fingers as Eunice had said. In the 30 minutes I had to myself while following her, I convinced myself I COULD do this. As we got to the house the smell of a delicious birthday meal was already present. She told me she was fixing lamb and hoped I liked it. She also said her Uncle Don and Aunt Erica had asked us to come for dessert later that night.

Wallowa Lake sits at about 5,500 ft elevation. Even though it was now July, it still was often cool. Kathy wanted a small fire built in the fireplace so I did this and we turned the loveseat to face the fire. As we visited I told her I had something to ask. She was curious as to what that would be. I started to say, "Would you...." "when it suddenly hit me that I had never told her I loved her. So I quickly shifted gears and said, "Before I say anything else I want you to know I love you. Now, I want to ask you to marry me."

Instead of getting a scream, a kiss and a "yes", I got a moment of silence and then the words something like, "Wow, I'll have to think about this. You have taken me totally by surprise. After my last visit there I thought you were coming up this trip and then you would be telling me good-bye." She went on to explain about our conversation about the girls coming and how she had translated my response to her. She thought I was growing cold about our relationship. Now I was asking her to marry me and she needed a little time to regroup. I asked her to please let me know by midnight that day. I wanted to know if my birthday was going to have a happy ending. She said she would do that.

After we had our birthday dinner we made our way to her aunt and uncle's home. They were and still are, very fun people. Kathy told them I'd asked her to marry me. They were excited until they found out she hadn't responded yet. They made her commit to calling them as soon as she decided. We got back to Kathy's home about 11:30 that evening. Kathy only had 30 minutes to make up her mind if I were to know before midnight. She said she had made a list. I had thought the list was about qualifications I might not meet. However, the list was actually three things she'd asked God to clarify about His future plans for her. She didn't know if marriage fit into them. I anxiously paced the living room while she went to her bedroom. About 11:55 pm she came out and said she'd decided. The answer is YES! She said God had confirmed for her that marrying me was completing the future plan He had for her.

We hugged and kissed and she said she loved me too. The next day being a Sunday, Kathy had arranged for many of her relatives in the valley to come to the lake house and have a potluck dinner there. She had done this as a nice social gathering so I could meet her many relatives. The nice thing was that now we got to tell them we were going to be getting married. We must have driven down to her folks that Sunday morning because I know we didn't tell them at the social. Kathy had wanted for me to ask her dad for her hand even though I had just turned 32 and she was soon to be 31. I don't recall his exact answer, but it was funny and to the point--something like--"hey, if she wants you, it's ok with me." He even offered to pay us to go to Vegas to get married. He said he felt that would be much cheaper than the church wedding he feared Kathy and her mom would arrange.

The next couple days were spent at the church camp where Kathy and I had arranged for and conducted all the music. It was a fun time which also allowed us to have a chance to drive into Pendleton to shop for rings as well as look at the calendar for an appropriate wedding date. We settled on Oct. 8 which worked into a time when I'd have a couple days off so we could have extra time for a honeymoon. Eunice was right all along-- Wallowa is beautiful in the fall!

The remainder of the summer brought the girls for their time with me in Idaho. Kathy came to Idaho to spend time with us and we went to Wallowa to spend time with her family there allowing Amy and Amber to meet their new grandparents who, by the way, became the kids' favorites. Grandma and Granddad Wolfe were to become the finest grandparents any children could have.

Kathy's birthday is July 23 and she was coming to Idaho for it. The girls and I had gone to a jewelry store where I bought a necklace that had tiny diamonds in the shape of a heart and a ruby in the center. Ruby is the birthstone for July so I thought it would be fitting for her present. I told the girls it would be a surprise for Kathy and showed them where I'd hidden it in my dresser drawer in the bedroom. The afternoon of the 23rd Kathy came driving into the yard. The girls went running out to greet her immediately yelling that they and dad had a big surprise and it was in the dresser drawer in the bedroom. They were pulling on each arm as they took her in the house and on to the bedroom. It wasn't how I'd foreseen her getting this gift, but how do you squelch young children's enthusiasm! I didn't and it turned out great.

The wedding came together and was wonderful. Kathy and I were very blessed with much love from both families--hers and mine. It might be a small thing to some, but it is a huge thing to me--what I want to share next. After my divorce my brother Ron had told me he didn't approve of my dating and possibly getting married again. He had been the best man at my wedding with my first wife and was now again the best man for my marriage to Kathy. Right after the ceremony Ron and I were walking from the sanctuary to the church's fellowship hall where they were having our reception. Ron stopped and hugged me starting to cry. He said he was very sorry for the things he'd said to me about marrying again. He was wrong and Kathy was the right person for me. I could have kissed my own brother right there for that very needed confirmation.

CHAPTER 12

The Secret is Out

Sometime in the spring of 1983 Kathy and I attended a marriage weekend. Kathy has always been one to enjoy attending workshops and conferences. I love this too so we usually agree about these. She is an avid learner following in her father's footsteps. I was eager to attend and actually, I don't even recall anything about it except this message: NO MORE SECRETS! We got home early Sunday evening of the weekend and I told Kathy we needed to talk. I then told her to get out her bags and pack them for when I finished telling her all I needed to say she would instantly want to leave. I didn't want this but I understood why she'd want it. She assured me she wasn't going to pack anything and I should just tell. I must have cried for an hour before I could finally talk between the sobs. I shared with her the years of abuse from Rich, what he'd done to me, the filthy person I was as a result of this, how I had these perverted thoughts about men, how I had dreams that tormented me and I just wasn't worthy of her. She needed to be set free from me. I never acted out on anything, but in my mind, it might only be a matter of time. This probably took a couple hours or so to share all that I did that night. I don't know for sure what Kathy fully thought, but all she said when I'd finished was, "If I had just told you all this about me, would you be leaving?" I said, "No, I had never thought about it in that light." She then told me I should get some professional help. She had sought counseling for some difficulties she'd encountered and it helped immensely. I wasn't sure about taking that step. Just taking this step had been a risk I thought I'd never take. I wasn't sure I could do this again. Surely God would provide healing for this now that I'd told my wife.

The next few years were ones of baby steps into sharing the truth of my past. The dreams I'd have at night were so vivid and tormenting that at times I'd not only awaken myself from the screaming and yelling, but I'd actually hit Kathy or kick her in my sleep. I was always being sought by an unknown being. I'd usually not see them but I'd be deep into jungle-like territory with my legs sinking deeply into what seemed like quicksand. The pursuer would be closing in on me and I just couldn't get away from him.

A couple years after our marriage we were taking Amy and Amber home after their summer stay. A friend of Kathy's had married a year after us and was living in Vancouver, Washington. We would drive through there on our return to Idaho so we spent the weekend with them. It was on one of these trips I stumbled into telling Lance, a pastor and husband to Jolene, Kathy's friend. Lance lived 400 miles away so I felt safer telling him. No one in Idaho knew him and besides, I liked him a lot and had begun to trust our friendship. He asked me lots of questions and ended the next day going to his office at church and getting two books for me to read. One

of the books was about a homosexual man who came out of
the closet. The next book was about a man who'd been the
victim of homosexuality and was coming out of the closet.
Kathy and I were on our way to the Oregon coast to spend a
couple days before heading home and my going back to work
for the new school year. I read both of the books in three days.
The one book sounded just like it would have been written
by my brother Rich from the standpoint of blatant steps of
homosexual acts he'd done. The second book was truly me.
This person was haunted by his frequent times of abuse and
the effects of the many years of it. I sent them back to Lance
thanking him for helping me so much. Now I had told Kathy
and I had for the first time told a man. Surely this would be
what God wanted me to do in order to bring healing for me
of this perpetual torment. Sadly, I was wrong. When I would
see Lance, he'd ask how I was doing and I'd usually say, "OK."

By now we had bought a home moving from the little
cottage farmhouse. We had seven acres and I loved it. I knew
Kathy was now fully awake to my background and was also
awakening to my behaviors stemming from this. I was in full
denial about my behaviors. I just saw myself as doing fine most
of the time. One particular Friday evening Kathy walked into
our living room from the kitchen. She asked me what was
wrong. I told her nothing was wrong. She said something must
be. I said again that nothing was wrong. She finally said, "Look
at yourself, something has to be wrong." I took a quick gander
of myself to see I was sitting on our couch in a fetal position
with my arms wrapped tightly around my legs. I repositioned
myself into a comfortable position and assured her I was fine.
It was then she asked me to talk with our own pastor.

Saturday morning I called Pastor Kay at his office thinking he'd not be there. Well, he was. I asked if he had time to talk with me and he said that would be fine. We only lived a mile and a half from the church so I was quickly in his office. I tried stepping into telling him all I'd shared with Kathy a few years earlier and also with Lance. Pastor Kay's response was rather different at the time. He knew I was principal of his youngest daughter's school and knew me from the work I did at our church as well as with the school district. He said, "Wow, you have really done a lot with your life considering your past. You should feel lucky to be where you are today. Many people with this type of background are in jail or prison." I assured him I felt lucky and went on my way. I know he didn't intend to leave me feeling like he did, but I wasn't strong enough to step any further into my story. If the truth was known, he actually made me feel guilty for not having a better handle on my issues. The fact that I should feel lucky to be where I was in life was a far-distant cry from my reality.

After Kathy and I had been married three years and having no success with her getting pregnant we started the process for adoption. Kathy, having never been married, wanted to have a child of our own. I was ok with this. I had had a vasectomy after Amber was born so after our first year of marriage I had a reversal surgery. We didn't know what problems we had, but after all the tests with her and me, adoption seemed the right next step. After all, we were getting into our mid-30's and we didn't want to be too old raising our family. We had also been looking into our going abroad for teaching in a foreign country. Kathy loved traveling and I'd always wanted to have this opportunity. Yet, if we were to have children, we wanted them to start their lives in America so we delayed for a year our pursuit of foreign work to see if God would open the door for a baby. The adoption agencies said it would be three to five years likely, but we also new God didn't have timelines. Ten months after we made our application to Health and Welfare's new adoption agency we had a call regarding a new baby. The mom had come to Caldwell due to her need to find safety from the baby's father. The agency considered the adoption a high risk. Because of this, the couple ahead of us on the list was not interested in the baby. Kathy and I saw this only as an answer to prayer. Our baby, Angela Frances, was born on July 7 and 20 hours later we were at the hospital to bring her home. Amy and Amber were with us for the summer so we had our entire family together for this wonderful arrival.

The Beginning of Help

With Angie at home, Kathy worked only part-time. There were predictable days when she'd be home. Thursday was one of them. This particular one I arrived home from school at about supper time. I saw a car in our driveway knowing it was one of our friends. I entered the living room where Kathy and she were talking. Stumbling into the conversation I overheard them talking about the friend's son and the struggle he'd recently had over a sexual matter between him and some other high school boys. She wasn't sure how to help him deal with it. Hearing what I did, I simply stated that I understood his frustration. This friend asked how I would know. I said I had been bothered by a brother older than me when I was growing up. She then asked what help I had received for it. I told her I'd had none but that I was really ok. That being said, I happened to see that Kathy had tears running down her cheeks. I knew those were tears of frustration knowing what I'd just said was a lie--I was not OK.

Seeing my wife's tears brought me to a point of true confession. I said to this friend I really wasn't ok. I knew I needed help but I was scared to share my past and furthermore I didn't have a clue where to go for help. She immediately told me of a male counselor she'd gone to see in Nampa. He was a Christian and was good. She gave me his name--David Myers. My first thought was--"Oh my word, in my earliest years of teaching I had a student with that name. I would be confessing everything to him--YIKES!" It didn't matter by this point. The next day I called the counselor's office and booked an appointment for the following Tuesday evening.

The weekend started with a phone call from my friend Mike Benedick on Saturday morning. He was wanting to borrow my rototiller. I told him that would be fine if he would come early and go into town with me. I was needing his pickup to haul some lumber to our house for a patio cover I was in the process of having built by my brother-in-law Sterling. Mike came right after lunch and we drove into Nampa. On the way I was on pins and needles. I was needing to talk with him about my upcoming counseling appointment. There were many reasons in my mind why I needed Mike to know about this--but telling him was going to take far more courage than I was able to muster on this drive into town.

When Mike had asked me to sing in his quartet back in college, he and I became good friends. During our college years this friendship was mostly around singing together which we did often. Even when our quartet wasn't singing, he and I did duet work together. After I had begun teaching at West Canyon in 1972, Mike had gone to California to pursue his medical degree. This didn't come together as he'd hoped so he moved back to Idaho and began a short teaching career as he regrouped. He would go in the summer time to Connell, Washington where his wife Carol's family lived. He would drive combine during the huge grain harvest taking place. This would usually last four to six weeks. This is where Mike and his family were in 1979 when my wife at the time told me she wanted the divorce. Mike and Carol knew nothing about this. However, while Mike was gone, God laid on his heart a scripture He wanted Mike to share with me. So, in the mail in early August, 1979 I got this note:

August 6, 1979

Earnie,

"May he give you the desires of your heart and make all your plans succeed. We will shout for joy when you are victorious and will lift up our banners in the name of our God. May the Lord grant all your requests."

Psalm 20: 4-5

Love,
Mike

I had thought at the time Mike must have known about the crisis I was in and he was being supportive. Later, much later, I came to understand he knew nothing, but God, of course, knew everything and prompted Mike to send me these encouraging verses.

When my second engagement ended Mike was again used by God to lift me out of Satan's quagmire. Mike was by now living in Washington where he was attending the University of Washington completing his medical degree in dentistry. He knew I was engaged but didn't know the day before I had been told of the rejection. In the mail I got a cassette tape of a song

God had laid on Mike's heart to send me. Little did he know the importance of its arrival and message. I was able to use the song many times in the days ahead to refocus me on what is important for God to hear from me even in my discouraging times. It also helped me to know that the power of Satan is often times a major cause of the torment we experience.

Mike had been prompted by God to reach out to me during the 2nd most critical time in my life of young adult years. It was because of God's use of Mike in my life that I wanted him to know about the upcoming counseling. I was so full of fear facing the telling of my past to an adult right here in the valley. He may tell me all kinds of things about myself that I feared were only true and then the word would get out.

As Mike and I got back to my house, we unloaded my purchase and loaded my rototiller in the back of his pickup. He started to leave when I asked if he'd take a minute to let me talk with him. Before I take this any further, I need to share one more experience with Mike that had reinforced my fear in sharing my past with him. While Mike was in Washington going to med school, he would come to Idaho for a short visit in the summer to see a brother he had in Boise. I was divorced at this time. He called and wanted to go out together and get caught up with one another. I happily agreed and we spent the evening together. As we pulled up to his brother's house where he was staying he reached across the seat and put his hand on my shoulder. He looked at me and said, "Earnie, I love you." That's all I remember. With this action, my translation was--"Oh NO, not Mike too!" Many times when Mike and I would sing together we'd make eye contact which for me was mostly about ensuring I was in time with him for I am not a person who senses rhythm very well and I need to know my lips are moving at the exact pace the ones I'm singing with are. However, now each time Mike's eyes and mine met, I had this awful sensation that I needed to be very guarded. Mike's eyes were always kind, but I knew perverted kindness.

Now we can go back to Mike and me having just loaded the rototiller in my pickup. I told him I was, the next Tuesday, going to go to a counselor. With that, I fell apart. I just started sobbing and couldn't stop. Between the sobs I began to let the dam break. I told Mike about Rich and his many years of sexual abuse, of dad's verbal and physical abuse, about when he had touched me and told me he loved me and the fears that left within me. Yet, in all of this I desperately needed the same friend God had used to help anchor me during my two rejections, to know about this most traumatic, forthcoming time. I needed his support. The amazing thing to me was what Mike showed at this time. Similarly to Kathy, it was only kindness, love and support. There was no rejection, no shock, no stepping away because he now knew I was "leprous and highly contagious". He simply expressed how sorry he was-- sorry for my misunderstanding of his love for me, sorry for the hurt and damage of my past and sorry it took so long for me to be able to share all this with him. He assured me he would be with me 100% of the time. This he did too. Mike drove right by West Canyon Elementary on his way from home to his dental practice. He would often stop by in the morning and leave me a note of encouragement, a scripture, and most of all a hug of assurance.

The Tuesday night of my first visit to David Myers came. I determined it didn't matter if this were a previous student. If he were a counselor and a Christian, surely he'd know what to do with me. I got to the office and waited to enter for my appointment. As I walked into Dave's office that first time I was flooded with relief! He had white hair! I was 39 years old now and the David I had as a student would be in his later 20's. White hair just wouldn't have been his hair color. My student had almost black hair. This David was in his early 60's.

We spent a few moments getting acquainted with one another. He quickly got to the heart of why I'd come. By now I was ready to spill my guts and live with whatever consequences I needed to face. I started by telling him about Rich and then dad. He confirmed I had viable reasons to come for counseling--I was needing to hear that. Seemingly in my mind I'd always been a "pansy" to dad. I didn't want to fight, I didn't want to wrestle, I didn't want to physically hurt someone in a sporting game--I was a pansy. To Dave I had been strong and resilient to have endured as long as I had without falling apart. He asked that first night if I had forgiven those who had hurt me. I assured him I had. I talked about Rich's death and that he'd come to my house a year or two prior to his drowning. I said that dad was dad and I was ok with him. He asked about mom. I said my mom was the kindest, most thoughtful person I knew. Why would I need to forgive her? He simply mentioned that moms usually step into things when their children are being hurt or misused. I told him I was good with mom. He asked then about God. I assured him God and I were good. Why would anyone need to forgive God? He's the King of the universe! He's the One who forgives us—me! Then he asked me a question that threw me for a loop. He asked, "Have you forgiven yourself?" With this I fell apart. I began to sob and sob. Of course I hadn't forgiven myself--how could I? I'd been the one who had gotten Rich beaten so badly for what he'd done. I was the one who actually enjoyed some of the touch Rich would do as I had gotten older. I was the one who had married the first time to hide my abuse so I could "look normal." I had used this relationship for all the wrong reasons. I had brought two children into this relationship too which God had to remove from me to give them safety. This was my fault--no one else. God had created me this way and I was stuck with this body and mind. Dad and mom simply had to raise what God had given them. These were all beliefs I was silently processing in my mind thinking they were real. I was just trying to make it through life without too much screw up and get into heaven where I could finally be "whole".

It was after this question and I finally got composure that Dave told me some "firsts". He told me I was not responsible for what Rich had done to me. Rich was. He said I was not responsible for dad's verbal abuse. Dad was. He said I was not responsible for the horrible beatings I'd received. Dad had an explosive temper. I may have deserved to be punished, but there was a difference between punishment and abuse. He mentioned that at some point we ought to talk about mom. Mom would have been well aware of Rich and dad's behavior. She could have said something to me. He then mentioned that God is King of the universe but this same God gave man a choice. I might need to address where I thought I stood with God and man's choices. After he said all this, he told me he wanted me to ponder all of this and then my homework for the week would be to write a letter of forgiveness to myself and bring it the following Tuesday. I was to read it to myself the next week in front of him.

An amazing thing happened at school the day after my first appointment with Dave. It was later afternoon and I was preparing to go home when one of my younger teachers walked into my office. She asked if she could talk with me and I said yes. She asked if she could shut my door and I said yes again. She proceeded to tell me she was seeing a counselor and he had asked her to share her story with someone she could trust. She had chosen me. She began sharing about how her dad had sexually used her from about the age of 10 until she left to go to college. He was a "church man". This would always take place on Saturday nights and they would all go to church together the next morning. Her mother never knew and still didn't. At this point she was crying and I was too. I shared with her I'd just had my first counseling appointment the night before and it was for similar reasons. I told her a bit of my own story. We began several months of "staying in touch". I have found God to be so good at bringing someone alongside when we need them the most.

The following weekend after my first appointment I went to our basement where I could be alone and began to struggle through the assignment Dave gave me. My word, what does one say to oneself in a forgiveness letter? I finally lit upon things like: "I forgive you for being the way you are." "I forgive you for telling dad about Rich." "I forgive you actually liking the touch Rich did at times." "I forgive you for marrying my first wife for all the wrong reasons." There were more, but these stand out in my mind some 25+ years later. As I read the letter to Dave the following week, I found myself beginning to realize for the first time that I had truly been a victim. Even though there was truth to what I'd placed in the letter, the truth was identifying some deeper issues I was still needing to address.

Over the next several weeks Dave took me through some work with dad and touched upon mom. Most of the time was spent with Rich. Before he did this he helped me create a safe place in my mind where I could see myself saying what I needed to say knowing no one would hear it except God and himself. I'd never heard of such a thing, but it worked well for me. I was so bottled up, I was ready to explode with most information he wanted or needed. In this safe place he had me go back in time to the starting of Rich's abuse. I could vividly see it. It was here, after several visits that he finally changed the scene. Up to this point Dave would have me picture Rich and me where the abuse happened. He would ask me if I could see anyone coming and, yes I could. It was Christ. I'd picture Christ helping me down from the place in the orange tree where Rich placed me. He would take me away from there. In this scene however, Dave wanted me to picture Christ going to Rich instead of to me. When this happened the picture went BLACK. I began to shake and even though it was June, I was shaking as though it were the dead of January and I was standing out in the weather naked. I was cold, clammy and scared to death! He asked what I was experiencing? I told him the best I could. His response startled me. He said, "I thought so." I asked what all this meant. His response was, this is about your relationship with God and you two need to work this out. Oh my word! Now I was up against the King of the universe. However, if this is what I needed to do, I would somehow do it. My appointments were always on Tuesday evenings so the next night was Wednesday night choir practice. It was early summer so I told Kathy when I got home from choir I wasn't going to come in the house. I was taking off somewhere. God and I had to have our time and get this squared away once and for all.

The following night was a beautiful early-summer evening about 8:30 pm. I had come home and intended to drive somewhere for this God battle. Because it was so calm and peaceful, I headed out on foot to the back of our property. We had seven acres. At the east end of it was a big irrigation canal. I walked to it thinking I'd walk the canal road until I was far enough away from anyone. I got to the canal to see that the grass had grown tall enough I could sit in it and be totally private. So, that is where God and I began our meeting. I sat there a while and finally said to God, "I'm feeling a little bit stupid sitting here trying to figure out what I should say to you." All of a sudden with that said I felt an enormous surge of emotion--full of bitterness and anger like I'd never felt before. I yelled, "I hate your guts for never coming to my rescue. You let Rich use me all those years, dad beat me up physically and verbally, mom never said anything and you, the King of the universe, did NOTHING! I was always all on my own." That being said I suddenly was surrounded with five people. They were Jesus, Dad, Mom, Rich and myself. I was still seated in the grass, but I was experiencing myself as part of this group and actually experiencing what was taking place in the group. For the first few seconds there was nothing said. All of us had our arms around each other's shoulders. I was between Rich and Christ. At this point Christ leaned his head between Rich and mine and said, "I want you to know Earnie, Rich never did what he did to you to hurt you. I also want you to know I love you."

Instantly, with hearing those words from Christ I started crying and felt this immense surge of cleansing throughout my inner self. It was the kind I'd heard others talk about when they had asked Christ into their hearts. For me, I'd always felt filthy inside. Christ was seemingly erasing this filth from me. I just cried and cried and then I was embodied in the person sitting in the grass. The key players were all gone and I was alone again.

132

I jumped up and ran to the house. I quickly, while crying, told Kathy of this miraculous experience! God had finally made me whole--I thought. All I could do was cry and praise the Lord. I went back to Dave the next Tuesday and told him I was healed! He said that was great but we probably ought to take a few more weeks to ensure my anchoring. I was sure I needed nothing but this healing and so ended the counseling for now. His last words at that time were, "If you find within the next year or two that there are some questions arising or new areas you discover, please let me help you with them." Little did I know the wisdom of this parting statement.

After this help from Dave I felt empowered to tell the world of my problem and how God had brought about such tremendous help. I didn't want ANYONE to suffer from past abuse and feel they needed to keep it in the closet. I had our pastor and his wife to our home the following Sunday evening to build a plan. I had thought I would use the pulpit to tell the entire congregation--They could be free! Pastor Kay felt the congregation as a whole wouldn't know what to do with much of my message. He said if I were ok with the idea, he would send people to me when they came to him with similar kinds of issues. He would greatly appreciate this kind of backup. I agreed to this and thus started a new step of ministry assistance I had never thought I'd be a part of.

One of the things Dave the counselor had told me to do was to start accountability in order to remain strong in stepping out into the world with a message like mine. I would find resistance and I'd find temptations I might never have had before. I talked to Mike about being this person and he said that would work for him. He'd appreciate having accountability himself. We started a weekly process of him coming to my office one day a week early in the morning on his way to the dentist office. We carried this practice forward for many years. Something I shared with him one day that had been troubling left me thinking I might need help beyond what accountability could offer. I've been told and read as such that most men will "self-gratify" to calm their sexual urges. I had developed this too. However, in my married life, I had continued it. Something I'd never been able to express was the fact that initiating sexual intimacy with my wife was always very difficult for me. The issues of Rich in my past always had to be processed through to get to the beauty of sexual intimacy with my wife. Thus, I'd wait and wait to ask and would sometimes just resort to self-gratification rather than stumble through all the anguish I'd have to work through. I don't recall just what I'd told Mike one morning but his response was a typical one--He said, "Oh, you shouldn't do that." Twenty-five years later, today, I'd use his comment as a discussion starter not letting it shut down the conversation we still needed to have. However, at that point I took it as a command. I tried to stop the habit, but I found I just couldn't and then, because I'd already told him, I now had a new secret. I'll write more about this as I get to the last section of this book.

CHAPTER 14

Parenting

Three years after Kathy and I adopted Angie, my oldest daughter Amy came to live with us. She had just finished 8th grade. She had talked with me several times about the possibility of living in Idaho with us. As much as I wanted this to happen I just couldn't see how I could separate her from Amber. The two of them were very close and I felt they needed each other. This particular year was different. Amy seemed desperate to move. So, a couple weeks ahead of school starting in the fall, I drove my brother-in-law Sterling's pickup to get Amy and her things so she could move in with us. She and Amber agreed this move was necessary in spite of their separation.

Having Amy come to live with us full time was what I thought--a wonderful change to our life. By now I had begun to recognize the fears I'd had early in their lives of hurting them like Rich had done to me or like dad had done were primarily gone and they were just FEARS. I had matured enough to realize those were their ways, not mine. What wasn't quite as wonderful was now having the parenting of a teenager and a three year old in our house. Amy was a great student so helping her focus on her classes was never an issue. However, having her focused on healthy relationships seemed more of a concern. Mostly, Kathy having only weeks of Amy and Amber living with us and now Amy full-time, was struggling. What was the role of a stepmom to look like and be like? What voice does a stepmom have with a high school freshman?

After the first year of Amy's living with us, Kathy came to me and said it wasn't working very well for her and wanted me to have Amy return to live in Washington with her mom and stepdad. I was really taken back by this. Kathy and I had by now been married six years but Amy was 14 and needed us. My response to Kathy was rather blunt, which some say I'm noted for. I said, "I have had Amy all her life and she had no choice about me. You made a choice to marry me. I wouldn't be sending Amy anywhere. You married me for better or for worse and this is part of the "worse". If you needed help being a step parent, maybe you should see Dave, the counselor who helped me so much." This was all Kathy needed to hear for her to seek help. It was the next week that she had her first appointment set. These appointments were not only good for Kathy but soon included Amy and me. All of us profited from his help and sage advice. Kathy and Amy were soon building a strong relationship.

Dave helped us learn to have weekly, family meetings. This gave Amy a chance to tell us when we were hovering over her too much and it gave us a chance to tell Amy when she wasn't being as open to us as needed. It even allowed Angie to have a voice which is so often overlooked when a child is only three. Kathy learned to set boundaries for our home. In the kitchen Amy would assist with chores and she was also able to earn money by doing additional chores.

CHAPTER 15

The Years Abroad

Kathy and I have always loved to travel. She had already been to Europe a couple times on her own prior to our marriage. I had always had it in my heart to teach abroad but had felt God wouldn't take someone tarnished like me and use me there. However, now I was entering a new era in my life. We began to check into teaching in China and other areas. Doors were open and our excitement began to build. Amy was part of these conversations too. She told us that going abroad was something she just couldn't do! With that Kathy and I agreed we would hold off from this planning until Amy's graduation from high school.

In late spring of 1992 Kathy's father had a second heart surgery. He'd been a smoker most of his life and this had done some damage. He'd had heart surgery in his mid-50's and was needing it again. He was 70 at this time. A well-known heart surgeon in Boise said he'd do the surgery. Everything went well for the surgery. However, when they attempted to take him off the respirator the following day his lungs were not strong enough to support his breathing. For nearly a month he was in ICU and eventually died from complications beyond anyone's control. It was a very hard time for all of Kathy's family. The Wolfe family had a couple of family corporations and Bill was the head of both. Relationships were strained at times with family members working details through. Kathy had been a peacemaker in this since we lived a couple hundred miles away and were not connected to the corporations like the three boys were.

It was during this time I received a call from a good friend who co-directed an international school in the country of Yemen. He was calling to see if there were any way Kathy and I would be willing to consider my taking a teaching job in the school and she being a bookkeeper for them? This was in October 1992. This was only four months after her dad's passing. Kathy couldn't even think of going at this point in our lives. We simply said we'd pray about it and see what God would do. Over the time Kathy and I agreed there were three things that would need to come together if we would go. Amy would go to a Christian college, Kathy's mom would give us her blessings and lastly, her one brother and one sister who lived close to her mom at the ranch would repair their strained relationship. We didn't share these with anyone except one another. They were our own prayer requests we felt God needed to answer. My own selfish one was that the school I had just opened for my school district would get a great principal replacement. I would be asking for a leave of absence if this were to come together.

Over Christmas vacation of that year Amber had flown down for time with us. We always took the kids to McCall, Idaho to ski and we were now on our way to McCall for this four day event. It would have been 7:30 am or so when we left our home. It was still somewhat dark as I pulled onto the highway heading north. From the back of our mini-van Amy said, "Mom and dad, I wanted to tell you I've decided I want to go to Greenville College, a private, Christian one. Kathy and I didn't say a word at the time but couldn't believe what we'd just heard. We had never had a conversation about this particular college, just the fact we wanted to help her all we could with college. This turned out to be God's first confirmation.

We were stunned to find God being so direct with His message about Amy's choice. She never waivered from this choice either. We flew her to Illinois over spring break that year so she could visit the campus and she came back confirmed this was the place for her to be. In the spring Kathy finally had to ask her mom if she would give us her blessings to go. Her words were very touching. She said she loved the Lord and if this is where He was sending us she sure didn't want to stand in the way. In spite of this second confirmation, Kathy had her misgivings of going because of the third one--the relationship restoration.

After we had been in Yemen only a month the confirmation came. Kathy received a letter from her mom. This letter was all about Kathy's brother and sister restoring a relationship that had been broken for nearly 15 years. Kathy cried with happiness. Both her brother and sister knew their mom needed them and how much she prayed for them to have a healthy relationship. Thus, they took the steps--God bless them both!

There was one other unexpected blessing God provided in this venture we were taking. I knew Amy never wanted to go abroad. However, her sister Amber was more adventurous like me. Amber was going to be a junior in high school and this would be a marvelous experience for her. The international school had an accredited high school so I knew she'd be fine there. She was a 4.0 student. I was stymied from asking because she was the only child at home for my ex-wife and her husband. Kathy told me I shouldn't be making this decision for Amber, I should let her do it. I only needed to hear this once and then called her. I asked if she'd ever consider taking this journey with us. She yelled, "YES, I thought you were never going to ask!" She needed to talk to her mom, but she definitely wanted to go. This was God's unexpected confirmation and blessing.

As we settled into life in a foreign country and the school, I felt the nudging from God to find accountability for myself. Kathy and I prayed for God's guidance in who to ask. There was a gentleman I worked with somewhat. His kids were similar in age to Angie and Amber, only more of them, and we had become friends. I talked to him and we began a weekly meeting. I shared with him why I wanted accountability to find he had in his heart sought this too but had never verbalized it. This lasted throughout our year in Yemen.

In the spring of the year I was asked by the organization running the school if I'd consider going to Turkmenistan to open the country's first international school in Ashgabat, the capitol city. Good grief, I'd never heard of it! Kathy and I prayed much about it and gave a tentative yes. We were able to talk to the American Ambassador in the country. His wife would be working with us at the school and we were told there was a Baptist missionary teacher also in the city who would likely join us bringing her few students to the school. We were told the country had little to offer anyone, but the people were the redeeming factor. This truly proved itself true. When our year was up with this country we wept as we flew away. Now, twenty years later, I still hold a special place in my heart for all the wonderful relationships we built in that one year.

I could write many chapters about our two years abroad but this book isn't for that purpose. There is one situation I want to share. As we got to Turkmenistan I was hoping to find accountability once again. I had wanted to pair up with an older gentleman who we quickly met. He and his wife were retired teachers living there working in the university teaching English to college students. They were seasoned Christians and I wanted to work with him. Kathy kept telling me I needed to pray about this as she wasn't confirmed in her heart he was the right choice. I had told her that her heart wasn't the one I was wanting to please--this was my need! Sound selfish or what! Having said this though, I knew I needed to pray about this. Kathy had told me she kept having another person come to mind when she prayed. I didn't have any misgivings about this. In the fall of the year I set a time to meet with this individual. I told him I'd like for him to consider being an accountability partner with me and touched on my story giving him some foundation as to why I was asking. His first response was--"Who talked to you?" I assured him it was only Kathy and God. He went on to tell me why he would very much like this too. It was unbelievable to me how in this remote country, God had already placed the person He wanted partnering with me for the year. For many years following our departure from the country, we stayed in touch. It was also another confirmation that a wife can be the very voice of God. He doesn't just use our ears and heart to speak to us.

CHAPTER 16

Returning to the US

The two years of my leave of absence were gone. Kathy and I needed to make a decision about staying in Turkmenistan or returning. I knew if we stayed I'd have to resign from my school district. With the leave of absence, they kept my seniority in place with a promise to a job for which I was certified. I was first asked to return to being the athletic director for our middle school. I told the superintendent at the time he'd never ask me about this position if he really knew me! I hardly knew the sporting seasons let alone the sport itself. With that I was given a 6th grade teaching spot.

We returned to the United States and reclaimed our home. We had rented it for the two years of absence. Lucky for us, God had given us renters who took care of it as well or better than we would ourselves. I came home, quickly planted some garden and tried to begin fitting into the culture of our country. We had been told the culture shock of returning was sometimes bigger than the one going. I found this to be true. My only culture shock in going was living in a very large city.

I'm a country boy and had never lived in town my entire life except my four years in college. Night noise and night lights were the most disruptive to me. It seemed there was never a peaceful moment. Peaceful for me meant absence of people with complete silence. I've always found great solitude in this. The two years in the city were anything but this.

Twice during the summer of '95, our return summer, my position changed for the school district. Finally, the second week of August I was placed back at West Canyon Elementary as the principal. The one who had replaced me when I opened the new school was leaving for a position in a neighboring district. I thought it would be like returning home. However, in the three years of absence from it, the classrooms had been closed off from the open classroom model and 80% of the staff was new. The only thing that remained much the same were the fine families that sent their children there.

Kathy and I were coming back to a church where we were very committed prior to our departure. Now we were like guests not sure where we would fit. Angie was going into fourth grade and needed a solid fit for herself. A redeeming piece for us was the news Amber had chosen to attend Northwest Nazarene University. She would only be 15 miles from our place. Our year in Yemen together was not nearly enough. There was a void when she returned to finish her senior year back in Washington. She had been given a presidential scholarship similar to the academic scholarship Amy had received from Greenville College. The president of NNU told Amber the reason he'd chosen her above others of equal academic strength was her decision to take her junior year and go to Yemen. He knew there was an inner strength of character in a student who'd do this and he wanted to honor that strength. I said, "Amen to that!"

I went to the associate pastor of our church wanting to know where we could be used. He told me he was wanting to begin a class for newly married for the church. We were getting several new couples with no place for them to get rooted in God's word outside of the pastor's message and no way to build strong relationships. We felt confirmed this would be a nice fit for us. Many of the couples we were told would be ones of second marriage and I was a second marriage even though for Kathy, it was a first. We asked another couple we had built ties with prior to going abroad to join us in this venture for which they did.

I'm not sure how many years we taught this class, but it grew from 3-4 couples at the beginning to 20-25 couples within a few years. We had to keep moving to larger classrooms. It was in this class I took a "bold step" for me. I don't recall the exact nature of the lesson that day, but someone had asked a question that led me to open up to the group about my childhood abuse and my need for accountability now that I'd had some counseling. Before that day was over I'd been asked by a couple of the guys if I would meet with them. Over the next 10 years I found myself meeting with no less than 20-25 different men in early mornings. The ones who were really stuck as I'd been I'd send to Dave and he would give them the same type of help God had used him to give me. This practice remained until I retired from the district in 2007.

I want to tell you about one particular person where my past being shared truly impacted him. This person had heard me share about my past. He and I had begun to meet somewhat regularly, but I hadn't shared the specificity of sexual abuse with him. On a particular Monday morning when we were to meet at 6:00 am, I arrived at 5:30 am to get to my office ahead of his arrival, have my coffee ready and my day focused. When I arrived at the school his car was already there. We greeted one another and walked into my office. He quickly said he had been there waiting because he had something significant to share with me.

He started by telling me his past had significance to it like my own. He had been sexually used as a child in different settings by neighborhood boys. This had haunted him for years. He had begun to act out by seeking sexual pleasure outside his marriage. This had been happening before their marriage and now it had begun after their marriage. The past night had been one of them. His wife had become suspicious, but he hadn't come clean with her. He was wanting to change but truly needed help. He also needed to tell his wife but was deathly afraid to confront the truth with her. We prayed and decided to do this together since they were part of the Sunday School class. I called Kathy and set a time for us to meet later that afternoon. He called his wife giving her the time we were to meet at our home where he'd share his truth in front of her with us being present. At the same time I also called Dave, my old counselor, to see if he had any openings for them that day. He did and so the plan was he would tell his wife and they would go see a counselor straight from our place that evening.

The plan turned into a reality that afternoon. I hadn't shared with Kathy what was being told. She and this man's wife were both hearing this truth for the first time. Kathy was able to be of comfort to his wife. Even though my story didn't have this type of acting out, it still had the depth of secrecy held back for many years. This couple went to therapy together for a few years and the young man had his own counseling separate of his wife. Little by little trust began to surface again. Lives were changed significantly due to their diligence, love for a common God, and a love for one another that wasn't ready to be severed by either of them.

I share this story with you because it is critical to know that God is never done working if we are only willing to let Him work. It does take a willing heart and a determination to not let retaliatory emotions get in the way of God's work and eventual forgiveness. Kathy and I can tell you much about this and so would this couple testify to this truth. The other truth I didn't know well at this time was just how much God uses our story to impact and empower others to take a step in finding health for themselves. This couple says they wouldn't be together today if God hadn't had us there. I know God is big enough that He would have used someone else if not me. But, God intended for me to grow too from my story being used. God does "use all things to His glory" as we give Him the opportunity.

The bold step of telling this Sunday school class a little about my past was a step I hadn't taken up to that point. My telling had only been in one on one situations. I was still gripped with the fear that if my community found out about my past they would not want their children to be under my administration. This fear was in part why I'd never stepped any further into administration. The role of superintendent was too public for me and too political. I wanted the safety of a single site where I could expend my energy assisting strong student learning without too much threat or fear.

CHAPTER 17

Secrecy's Last Years

When our youngest daughter was going into her high school years she was experiencing some difficulties around her position in our family and who she was as a person. Kathy understood this to connect to the fact she was adopted, but that understanding didn't help us deal with the acting out we were experiencing. We went to see my counselor friend, Dave. At the end of this session he took me by surprise and asked if I'd ever confronted my father about the issues I'd shared with him. It had been 10 years since I'd talked to Dave about dad but he hadn't forgotten the significant hurt. I told Dave I hadn't done this. I also said that dad was now in a nursing home and was struggling with much dementia. I wasn't sure I could even have a sane conversation with him. Dave's parting words to me were, "It is a lot easier to confront someone in life than it is in their death." I concurred with his thinking and we left.

As Kathy and I were driving home from Boise where Dave lived I said to Kathy, "How come I have to confront dad when I've always been one to stand up for him when my other siblings would cut him down? Kathy's response set me straight. She asked if I recalled using the term "those are just Harold's words coming out". I said of course I recalled using this statement. I used it whenever I did something that would be stinging to someone in how I talked to them. Kathy said, "Well, you may think that saying it's a "Harold" might make someone forgive you. But for most people, they don't even know who Harold is. All they see is you." I told her thanks for making this clear. I knew I'd have to confront dad and the sooner the better.

I began to pray a lot about how to talk with dad and what to say. I knew the dementia would make this extremely difficult but I had to try. I made about 50 different speeches in my head, but finally relented to just—"OK, God, this is your time. I'm going to say what you lead me to say and I'll rely on you." This was a key ingredient.

On Sunday I went to see dad which I often did on Sunday afternoon. Dad didn't get too many visitors. He'd destroyed so many relationships with family that few wanted to see him. Those of us who did visit did it more out of obligation rather than desire. He was a 94 year old man wasting away. When I arrived he called me by name and seemed quite coherent. I told him I wanted to talk about some things in the past. He seemed fine with that. I started to say things about how hard I'd tried to please him but how different I was from him. I never felt he liked me much. We had a great 45 minute conversation with dad saying he'd liked me and respected me.

The second visit the following Sunday found dad in a similar state as the previous week. This time I told him I wanted to talk about Rich. I asked if he recalled the time I told him that Rich was going to my bed at night and doing things to me. He emphatically remembered this! He told in great detail how he'd BEAT him. These were his own words. He then went on to say that he didn't seem to get it. Once the beating was over, Rich seemed to have a blank stare about him. I told him that two weeks after that Rich had started coming to my bed again. This continued until I was 16, another 5 years. I never told dad because I wasn't going to be responsible for Rich getting beaten so badly again. Dad said he was sorry about this but had done what he'd thought best. I wasn't sure this is what I was wanting to hear but I really didn't have any expectation except to tell him.

The third week came and dad was very coherent yet again. This time I asked him if he remembered telling us boys when we were young about our Uncle Eri. He was one of dad's older brothers. Evidently my grandpa Lewis was a very strict, abusive father, just like dad. Uncle Eri had never forgiven him and said that he hated his dad. This had always been troubling to my dad and he had tried many times to get Uncle Eri to forgive their father. I'm told he did finally do this only days before his death. Dad took at least 15 minutes to tell me many stories about his dad and Eri confirming this truth. At that point I said to dad, "You know the way Uncle Eri felt about your father is the way I feel towards you." Dad got really quiet at this point. I went on to tell him that from the time I'd been a small child I'd tried and tried to be the one son who did what was right, not rebelling and not running away. No matter how I tried you didn't seem to care. You beat me up physically until you couldn't any longer and then you used names and stinging insults to "break my spirit". In all my singing I never got a compliment, instead I'd get cut down for "getting the big head". When I was in college and came home to tell you I'd been elected class president and you wanted me to decline so I'd still come home. I told you I'd still come home and you pushed me out saying you never wanted me to come back. I came back anyway because it was the right thing to do. No matter what I did, it wasn't good enough for you. Today I hate you for this. Dad was very alert at this point and took my arm with his two feeble hands. He said, "Earn, I'm sorry. I guess I told everyone but you how proud I was of all you had done." He went on to say of all the kids I had been the only one he never worried about. I would always be home when I said I would or sooner. I never challenged what he or mom had said was the right thing to do. Yet in all this dad had never once told me until now. I cried and he did too. I felt released when I left the nursing home that day. Two months later, dad died.

The afternoon I was called by my oldest sister saying the nursing home had just called and dad had slipped away in his sleep, I told Kathy I had to get into the nursing home before they took dad's body away. I drove in quickly and found they had placed dad's body in a back room awaiting the mortuary to arrive. I asked to go where his body was. I took his hand and told him there that I loved him and thanked him for being my dad. I'd never said either of these to my dad in all my years. I hadn't forgotten all the troubled times, but I knew dad had done the best he knew to do. No, he didn't corral his anger, temper, moodiness, and pride, but he was my dad. He and mom had given me life and they'd also given me the siblings I loved and adored. For this, I thanked him.

In 2007 I reached the year where I could retire from public education. In retirement God had a significant step He was wanting me to take. I didn't know it yet, but HE DID. I was actually retiring so I could step into some educational consulting. The Dean of Education at the College of Idaho in

Caldwell and I had sent off three grants for supporting the re-establishment of a professional learning center at the college. I would direct this center--we thought. By August of the summer of 2007 when I had retired, the last grant fell through. We only needed one of the three to fund it. Kathy and I had planned to go visit our kids in Oklahoma the last couple weeks of August so we went having no idea what I would come back to. Upon our return I had a couple calls on our answering machine. One was from the Center of School Improvement at Boise State University and the other from the Idaho State Department of Education. Each was wanting a meeting with me to talk about working with some projects they had in mind. Over the next couple weeks I agreed to much of the work they had outlined. The work God was wanting me to do was already being taken care of. I learned a lot about trusting the unknown from that time.

Prior to my retirement one of Kathy's brothers had talked to her and me about a ministry he was now involved at his church in Western Oregon. It was called Celebrate Recovery. I had privately shared a sliver of my childhood with him. He thought this ministry would be something I'd not only enjoy, but might be a good fit for our church. In inquiring about it the early summer of '07 I found a day training was being held in Boise at a church that had it in place already. The Saturday after my last day of work, Kathy, two other couples from our church and I attended this day long training. All of us were intensely interested in getting this going. I knew it would be the right next step for me to help others step out of their closets.

PART III

Finding Freedom

PREFACE

It has been surprising to me to get to the third part of this book's writing and discover the most difficult part is this section. Somehow, all through my life, I've wanted to get to freedom. Freedom would mean just what scripture says: "to be free indeed!" It would also mean as I've stated so many times-- "to be normal". No one told me that being free meant free from bondage but not free from memory or residual effects. Nor does it mean to be free from any further temptations in life. God has pointed out to me numerous times how he wants my "mess to be a message". That has always been fine with me. I just kept thinking things like temptations would be gone. I am learning that with maturity comes wisdom and so I'm understanding that this Godly freedom has a cost factor. With this said, as I go into this last section on finding freedom, I'll be defining what this cost factor is like.

A very significant finding has happened for me in this path to freedom. The main one has been finding my identity and what that actually means. Because the abuse started so young with Rich and dad, who I am has always been completely interwoven with the effects of abuse. I could never say, "I had this belief at this or that point in my life because that's when the abuse started." Instead, I've found myself stepping into the realization that I gain steps to freedom at this point of my life because God is helping disconnect the effects of abuse from my actual identity. The fear I've always carried that I will be dad or be Rich is only a fear. As God is remaking me into more of His image, I pull further and further away from the idea I was predestined to repeat what they did or who they were.

Another reality I've been discovering is just how selfish fear is. Without any intent on being selfish, I've discovered that being fearful places the lens of myself on me. I use to say things like, "Oh, that was a Harold coming out of me." I'd think that was funny. My wife finally awakened me when she informed me that most people in my life don't know Harold. The behavior is mine and they only see me. I might be genetically predisposed to behave or respond/react a certain way. But, I CAN choose to address this in me and work to change it. Dad didn't do this. I can. His pattern of behavior doesn't have to be mine and the farther I get down the road of freedom, the more I realize I'm not even like him (most of the time). The same holds true for Rich. The fact I have thoughts resulting from the abuse certainly doesn't mean I'll act on any of them. I never have. I can always choose. This reality is very freeing unto itself.

An element that Celebrate Recovery has taught me comes from the Serenity Prayer. We end each session with the recitation of it. There is a sentence towards the closing that goes, "Taking one day at a time, enjoying one moment at a time, accepting hardship as a pathway to peace...." Learning to discipline myself around this phrase has been hugely beneficial for me. Because my whole life, in my mind, had been so influenced by the childhood abuse, I had never realized the importance of taking only a day at a time. The scripture I already knew about "don't be anxious about tomorrow" was important but not something I could put into practice. As I consciously worked recovery steps, I began to address "taking one day at a time". As I did this I then began to understand "one moment at a time". There are many days when I have one battle after another. If I choose only to take the present battle keeping my mind on it and releasing any anxiety to God about what may be coming next, I can relax so much more. The last part of the serenity prayer says "accepting hardship as a pathway to peace". No matter how difficult the circumstances are, if I let God be in control and thank Him in advance for the work He's doing even when I can't see anything, I CAN find the "pathway to peace". Now, just because I've written this here doesn't mean I've mastered it. It does mean however, that I'm cognizant of it much more that I've ever been before. The biggest discovery about "accepting hardship as a pathway to peace" has been thanking God for the hardship and what I will learn from it. Praising God and Thanking God for difficulties is never easy. In fact, until more recent years, I thought it was a little delusional. However, I've found that in praising God, I release my anxiety and fear to Him KNOWING he will use all things to His glory. This is perfect trust when we can do this ahead of the outcome. When I awaken in the middle of the night with anxiety I will finally be able to find sleep again when I am able to thank God for what had awakened me knowing He is already working on it.

I've sung the song "We Are More than Conquerors" many times in my life. I've often wondered what being more than a conqueror meant? I'm now beginning to understand some of this. When one conquerors, there had to have been a battle being fought and ultimately won. However, the battles I've faced for much of my life were not battles I needed to fight. They were battles already won.

The significance of my battles already being won hadn't been recognized. I was fighting them on my own not knowing this team: God, Jesus and The Holy Spirit had conquered them already. Now, and only now, am I understanding that "I am more than a conqueror" can mean I am the recipient of a conquered battle I didn't even have to fight. It was done for me. When we finally realize this as I am beginning to, I can praise His name for I am Free!

One last piece, before I walk you through the steps I am taking to find freedom, is my awakening to the fact that I'm not so different after all from others around me. I've said repeatedly in this book that I was a gardener, singer and educator. I had to do them really well so I'd not be like dad or Rich. I hate to confess this, but I HAD, in my mind, to outdo those two in order to not be like them. What I didn't realize was the way I appeared to some people around me. Some people have thought I was a "goodie boy". In fact, one lady in our church, following the introduction I gave of my past when we introduced Celebrate Recovery to our congregation, told me she was ashamed of herself. She always saw this smiling face of mine as one that never knew pain. She thought that if I had her past I wouldn't appear to be so happy. She asked my forgiveness. I told her I had always HAD to put on that face so others wouldn't know my truth. Little did I understand until now how important it is to turn all of this over to God one day at a time, one moment at a time. He turns our hardship into a pathway to peace. A surprise for me is that I continue to smile whether I think I need to or not. I love laughter. I love creating it as well as experiencing the fun and humor in it.

CHAPTER 18

Second Step

Our church was in the process of getting a new senior pastor the summer of '07. I had met with him to acquaint him with Celebrate Recovery hoping he'd know about it already or want to give support to it. He seemed genuinely interested in our taking this step. He encouraged me to keep working with it and let him know what steps the church would need to take to support it. After the day training we had attended, I ordered all the leadership materials I was told was needed for it. I began that summer reading through it. In doing so, I got more and more convinced that I was not the right person to lead it--I NEEDED IT! I couldn't lead what I was desperately needing to experience myself. I think it was September of 2007 when I went to our pastor and told him my dilemma. He then told me he'd heard of a gal in our congregation who was leading a ladies' recovery group. He suggested I ought to talk with her and see if she knew of this program. The gal's name was Carol Garmire. Carol Garmire! I thought! My word, I graduated college with her, she had taught in a neighboring school district all our years, her kids had gone through my school, she and I use to sit by one another in chapel in college because in those days we had to sit alphabetically. Her maiden name was Ladder and mine being Lewis put us often beside one another. How could I know so much about her and not know she was leading a recovery group? I called her and set a time for Kathy and me to come and meet with her and her husband Lonnie.

The meeting between Garmires and the Lewis' took place in a couple days on a Thursday night. I told Carol and Lonnie about Kathy and I attending the Celebrate Recovery day event and our interest in getting this ministry off its feet at Deer Flat. I also told her briefly of my background and that I could not see myself leading this--I needed it. I then asked if she'd have any interest in joining this effort. Little did Kathy and I know that Carol and Lonnie had been praying about what to do with their energy to support God's Kingdom. This seemed to possibly be the right step for them. Carol had already attended a recovery program and had also attended a Celebrate Recovery in a neighboring town. She herself was already qualified to take a group of us at Deer Flat through a leadership training. Lonnie had said he wasn't sure this was for him having not been through any recovery program himself, but I assured him I needed him there for moral, personal support. He said that was enough for him and he'd go.

Carol and I arranged with our pastor to have a short segment in front of the two morning worship hours and introduce this potential ministry for our church. We each gave a short testimony of what brought us to this point in our lives. It was a huge step of faith for both of us. I had never told this much to several hundred adults. From this introduction we had seven potential leaders willing to start meeting weekly. In order to be qualified to lead Celebrate Recovery one must go through a crash course of the entire curriculum taking all the steps recovery requires. This is what Carol was qualified to do and so she took the other six of us through these steps. A kink we encountered in doing this was finding a sponsor. A sponsor is to be someone of the same sex as you. They have to have gone through all the steps themselves and found sobriety in at least one area of their struggle to qualify for being a sponsor. We had no one qualified except Carol to sponsor someone. Four of us in leadership were men. We got permission from our state Celebrate Recovery representative to start with Carol as our initial sponsor and when we had others qualified, we would switch over to them.

I wanted to tell this little kink because it was a gift from God for me to have Carol rather than a man as I began. My abuse had all come from men. The sexual abuse had come from one of my brothers and the emotional/physical abuse from my dad. My trust to share such deep issues kept me hugely reserved with men. I always feared a couple things: one, if people found out they'd think I'm not trustworthy and secondly, if I opened up to a man, he may be like Rich and know I was "easy prey". So, having Carol, someone I'd known much of my life as my first sponsor, was a huge relief for me.

From January to August of 2008 Carol took the group of fledgling leaders through the steps. In August we went to the Celebrate Recovery Annual Summit at Saddleback Church in Southern California. This was the best investment we made next to the initial investment of being willing to step into this. At the Summit we were able to meet with all the areas needing addressed in the ministry. It is almost a church within a church. It has its own weekly dinner, worship, lesson or testimony and then an hour of share time, and lastly, a dessert to close out the night. This is all required to be called a Celebrate Recovery. It is what is called the DNA of the program. One never waivers from this so that safety is built into the program. No matter where you are meeting in any state or in any country the structure is the same as well as the components within the structure.

About a month before going to the summit we had gotten permission to speak to the congregation at our church to see if any would want to financially help support our attendance at the summit. It was going to cost each one of us about $750.00 apiece. Some of us didn't have the funds. We gave our speech and had never heard that any money was donated. We stepped out in faith with six of us attending. While we were there I wanted to call our church office to see if there was any money available to assist with some material purchases we needed to make. While on the phone I was told we had $3,500 we hadn't used so yes, there was substantial money available. I asked where that had come from. I was told it was given the Sunday Carol and I had asked for donations. Different ones in the office had thought the other one had told us. At that point I didn't care. I was overjoyed! I went to tell the rest of our group and we all praised God for this. We were able to buy all we needed to start up and to reimburse those of us who had paid for others not able to cover their own expenses.

Going through the Celebrate Recovery program the first time in order to be qualified to lead it hadn't brought about the freedom I was hoping to find. (Remember, I wanted to be normal, free from temptation and free from acting on any temptation). I had always had the dream that someday all of my past would be erased and I'd be "normal" just like I thought everyone else was. I then knew I needed to go through the program as it was intended taking the necessary time to address all the steps thoughtfully and timely. I was leading worship for CR, leading a share group and co-leading a men's step study. In doing all this I was seemingly getting worse (to me) instead of getting better. I wasn't struggling less, I was actually struggling more. Now people knew the truth about me and I wasn't better. I still wanted to escape life and go into pornography or crawl into a corner and escape people. I loved what I saw others experiencing, I just didn't find it for me.

Kathy and I have a second home in McCall, Idaho which is a little resort town in the mountains of Idaho about 120 miles north of where we live. In June of 2009 we used our home as a retreat site for our growing leadership group. We were wanting to reflect on our year's efforts and see what we needed to adjust or change. We started with some training on Saturday morning. After that I had everyone give a personal reflection of their first year. There were approximately 12 of us present. I was going to be last just because I was taking charge of this portion. I was listening to everyone's statements of growth and feeling more condemned with every person's words. By the time it got to me I started by saying I appreciated how much everyone was growing. However, I needed to resign from leadership because a leader needed to be sober and I wasn't sober from the one item I thought I'd come to Celebrate Recovery to address—porn. I didn't flee to it all the time but I did flee to it at times. This, however, wasn't sobriety. I broke down and cried at this point. The group was quickly taken over by Carol who had everyone gather around me and pray. Then she told me we would talk. That didn't happen until the next morning.

I am an early riser so I was up between 5 and 6 am. Later when Carol came into the living room she asked for me to join her. She took me to the corner chairs where we sat. She said she had seen many times my difficulties through the past year. She also reminded me I had been calling her regularly about them. This is a healthy relationship between a sponsor and sponsee. She said I was not dropping out of leadership. I was setting the right example as a leader. She said the fact I was attending CR without missing a week for a year was the first step of sobriety and I was going to take a "one year chip" for this. This chip would represent that I was stepping out of denial and staying sober to the fact I needed help. Up until this point I wasn't taking any chips for sobriety. She then said something that sent me in a whirl. She said she felt I was never going to find the sobriety I wanted from porn until I went back to counseling. In Celebrate Recovery we address three things: Hurts, Hang-ups, and Habits. I was addressing a habit without getting to its root cause—Hurt. She felt the deep hurts of the abuse were still there. I knew it was true but was hearing dad's voice about addressing hurts. A man is tougher than that—saying this out loud only made me the "sissy" dad said I was. In my head I knew better than this, but in my emotions I felt like a wimp. By this point in my life my first counselor, Dave, had retired and was no longer seeing clients. However, Kathy and I had met and worked with a new counselor off and on whose name is Judy.

We had gone to Judy for different reasons over a few years—things like parenting and intimacy in marriage. I'd take on assignments to try to overcome my response to intimacy only to be good for a few days/weeks and as soon as possible resort back to my distancing from touch. We had assignments where we were to sit by one another on the couch, hold hands in public or walk close to one another. One particular example I'll give here is when Kathy, our youngest daughter, Angie, and I were going to a concert at Boise State University. Kathy and I were coming off a counseling session where I was to hold hands in public. So, after we got out of the car in the BSU parking lot I took Kathy's hand. We were walking towards the building when Angie, who was walking behind us said, "Good grief dad, if you are going to hold mom's hand then walk beside her!" I instantly looked at us and realized I was about 3-4 feet away and my arm was outstretched to Kathy's hand. We did look foolish but I hadn't had a clue until then. Kathy said she was accepting this, thinking I was "learning". In reality, I was tolerating.

CHAPTER 19

Three Years of Counseling and Therapy

The first couple sessions I set with Judy, counselor, were with Kathy attending. Somehow, I thought we should do this together since our marriage was being impacted by my responses to life. After two sessions Judy suggested she and I meet a few times alone so she could become more familiar with my background. This turned into almost three years. We spent several weeks talking through the abuse from Rich and from dad. She pressed some points like Dave had done about my feelings toward my mom and towards God. She was more insistent that we take time addressing both of them. Judy, being a mother herself, felt I needed to step into this with my mother. This was literally taking place 20 years after I'd had counseling from Dave. Talk about being stuck!

The thing I was beginning to see from meeting with Judy was the difference between exposing abuse for the first time and the initial trauma to now going deeply into the abuse for the sake of identifying it and beginning to overcome the damage. When I'd met with Dave I was extremely driven to become a whole person—a normal person. I wanted this to happen as quickly as possible too! I had been told by my first counselor, Dave, I may need to return for further counseling. Little did I know at the time just how much he understood that I didn't. Twenty years later and this normal person still not being found, I was realizing I needed to back fully away from trying to set a timeline for me. I remember telling Judy during one particular session that I wanted her to tell me when she thought I was "healed" as I did not have a means of doing this. She assured me we would do this together.

In the early months of the counseling I was having my morning devotions. I was reading in Ezekiel 24:26 which says: "I will give you a new heart and put a new spirit in you; I will remove from you your heart of stone and give you a heart of flesh." (New International Version) I remember journaling that morning asking God what a heart of flesh was like? When I had accepted Christ in my heart as a boy I remember seeing in my mind a heart that was sparkly clean like the stainless steel milk buckets looked right after we had sterilized them. I use to think that was the cleanest look one could find. This scripture was now saying God would remove a heart of stone and give a heart of flesh? As I journaled God told me that He was doing that for me. I was waking up to the fact that I had a hardened picture of my heart. My heart was damaged just as my body was. God, being my Healer, was going to give me a heart of flesh. I didn't have any idea what this would mean. I was cautiously excited however to find out. I began to find that my heart is alive and that it can grow. This is a heart of flesh. Somehow, I'd believed I needed to harden my heart. I was soft. That's why Rich could use me, why dad would say I was girly-like crying over TV programs or movies. Hardening my heart was a necessity. Because of the misconception I had of my heart, I thought a clean heart was like the steel bucket. Yes, one can sterilize a bucket, but you can't change it and grow it. Little by little God has shown to me that a heart of flesh is one that is alive and well. My identity has increased for the good as my awareness of my heart of flesh increased. The original Earnie was OK as God had made him. The problem all along had been with dad and Rich. This heart of mine is also the home for The Holy Spirit whom Jesus gave me when I received Him into my heart. The Holy Spirit was not able to have real freedom with me as long as I lived with the thinking that my heart was one of stone and not of flesh. God, all this time, was waiting for my readiness to this reality. God's Holy Spirit just wouldn't find a stainless steel bucket as a great home within me. A new heart meant a living, growing heart.

About six months into the counseling Judy asked for permission to use some new training she had recently gone through. It was a therapy used for PTSD—Post Traumatic Stress Disorder. I had only briefly heard of this at the time from its successful use with vets and their trauma from war. She told me there were different levels of therapy she could try and wanted to know how aggressive I wanted her techniques to be. I told her I had lived with this so long I wanted her to go for it with the most aggressive means she had. I'm not going to try and explain all that took place during this time, but I will go deeply into some of the situations that resulted during this therapy.

The first session where therapy was being applied, I could not believe the seemingly thousands of flashbacks I was seeing. For a moment I felt shocked that these very real events from my past were still able to be recalled and be recalled so vividly. I always had a focusing assignment for the therapy. It seemed we stayed with the topic until I simply "lost it". I'd begin to sob uncontrollably. The therapy would stop and Judy would patiently wait. I'd be asked to tell what I had experienced and interestingly, where I felt the pain of it. I was to learn that the agony of hurt is stored in different places in our bodies. I had seemingly maxed out my body's storage tanks in all areas. There are two incidents I want to bring into this book. They are significant in my finding a fuller recovery.

The first session I'll write about is when my assignment was to begin to find "little Earnie". She kept asking me about him and I'd talk about things that had happened, but I just had no emotional connection to him. I had no idea the disconnect I created between my early years and their emotional hurts and my current years. I knew the hurt of the event I might talk about, but I had no emotional connection to the day to day boy I was at that time. In this particular therapy session I recall seeing myself very young in a vivid memory and actually feeling the emotions I'd had at that same event. I actually thought this was a rather "fun moment". Feeling emotions other than bitterness or hatred toward much of my younger years was nice.

The following morning I was up early having my morning devotions. I'd read my devotional, read my Bible and was now going to start my journaling. When I opened my journal I instantly saw something that perplexed me. I had this colorful image come to mind. It was of a young, small lad in bib overalls standing on a dirt path with a pasture and barbed wire fence around it. The boy was all alone, standing there with this path in front of him. He didn't look scared, just was there. I instantly knew who this was. It was ME. I immediately knew I was about to take this boy on a journey—this path in front of him. As the adult Earnie, I also knew the pain of this path and I simply could not envision taking this boy through this again. The path in front of this boy didn't appear threatening, but I KNEW where the path led and so I could not let this happen. I did some journaling about this, had my prayer time—mostly pleading time that God would not let this happen. Then I went and got Kathy. We were walking most mornings at this time and it was now time for the walk.

As we started I told her about seeing little Earnie this morning and the struggle I knew he was about to face. Having said that much, I began to cry. For the next 45 minutes we walked and I tried to explain what I was encountering. How in the world could I take what I knew had already happened to me (to the little boy) both by Rich and dad, and make this little fellow experience it all over again?! What good could such torment do? I was in such a state of agony Kathy asked if I wanted her to stay with me that day. She was going to work at Symms' Fruit Ranch where she did some part-time accounting. I assured her I'd be fine. I just needed to get this off my chest and I had done that the past 45 minutes walking with her. Her parting words were that I should think about calling Judy, the counselor.

As soon as Kathy left, the haunted thoughts started again. I thought that maybe calling my daughter in Oklahoma would give me the needed diversion. So, I called Amber. She answered and we said our routine "how are you" and I then started to tell her about seeing this picture that morning of myself when I was young. Amber was aware I had been going to counseling but living 1,500 miles away kept her from knowing too much detail. I started to give her some detail when I lost it all over again. I just couldn't get a grip on this. Amber questioned several times if I were ok, and I assured her I was--just needing to get this spoken out loud and thanks for listening to me. I hung up hoping I was right. I wasn't. Within the next 20-30 minutes I knew I had to call Judy.

I had not made it a point to call Judy in-between my weekly visits. She's a busy counselor and I knew she sure didn't need this wimp of a grandpa calling to ruin her morning. But, I did it anyway. She answered and I apologized for disrupting her time. She assured me it was fine and with the deep therapy we had been addressing she wasn't surprised that I needed to do just this. I stepped into telling her what had taken place during my devotional time. She fully understood and confirmed I had indeed seen myself and had a first awakening of connecting emotionally with me in my early years. I told her my fears of taking him through this. She asked if he were afraid? I had no idea. I said I thought he was just innocent but didn't need to take this journey through such hell all over again. I told her I didn't know what to do.

Judy's response to me was such a huge next step. She just said, "Why don't you let him tell you what he wants you to know?" I asked how in the world would I do this. She told me to put a pencil in my non-dominant hand and let him ask his questions or speak his comments and I'd write them down. I would then respond to them by shifting the pencil to my dominant hand and respond. I had heard of this type of therapy and thought it was a little quirky, but here I was now being told to use it. I was desperate enough that I didn't care how quirky it seemed, if it would only work.

I went into our den where I do my devotions each morning. I took my journal and wrote:

May 30, 2009 Jesus, my dearest friend and brother. I am so glad --beyond words--for what You've done for me. I am, I think, at a crossroads--however, I won't believe this until it's confirmed by someone other than me. Now that I have found my little self and we are recognizing ourselves as one, I can begin to walk this path with him until we are one. This path is my life already lived. This time I will walk it with you (little Earnie), with God and Jesus and my newest Friend, The Holy Spirit. So here we go.

At this point I put the pen in my right hand (I'm a lefty) and this is what came out of it:

What is Rich doing? Why does he take me to the trees? What's he doing to himself? Who is that with him? Why does he want me? I don't like this!

I was amazed to have these questions come out of me from a part of me I hadn't ever been in touch with prior to this moment. I took the pen in my left hand and wrote back to little Earnie:

Rich is going to use you sexually. Rich is troubled and he thinks he needs you to fulfill his sexual desires. He takes you into the trees so he is safe from anyone knowing. He's not aware he is troubling you so. Rich feels safe with you so he trusts you. Rich is masturbating while he is touching you. (This is really offensive for me to write). He's pleasing himself with no understanding or regard for the damage to you. The "someone" with him I don't know at this point. I suspect it is the neighbor boy who use to chum with Rich but I'm not sure. Just between us, I wonder if it could be Jesus. He's been so close to me as I go through my help. I know you don't like this for I hate knowing this happened to us. What's amazing is you're still here within me and we are for the first time having this conversation about all this. Praise be to God. I love you--little me. Thank you Judy. Thank you Jesus, dearest Father and Holy Spirit.

What was so astounding to me as I wrote little Earnie's comments and then my own back to him was the ease in which it happened. Little Earnie wasn't stressed as he wrote nor was I as I wrote back. It was as if I were talking to someone deeply interested in hearing what I had to say about their question, but doing so with two humans rather than this type of scenario.

As the days and weeks rolled on little Earnie and I communicated daily through this journaling process. In fact, the following day he asked me why he wet the bed and sucked his thumb? I was able to tell him that he wet the bed because of great trauma within himself. The actions of Rich and the fear of dad don't let your body respond to the natural things like waking up when you have to go to the bathroom. Sucking your thumb is a safety thing you do to help yourself feel better. This therapy became a genuine source of healing for me. It was one of the first steps of helping me feel like a whole person.

I'm going to step out of the timeframe of this counseling to write what is happening currently with me in the process of writing this book. I truly was amazed to come in touch with little Earnie during the therapy six years ago. I have already stated that the emotions I felt in experiencing little Earnie were about amazement in the fact that I'd actually felt me as a child. I had thought I'd get all kinds of intense reactions from him rather than simple questions that were more curious that traumatic. I still believe this is the case. So, what I want you to know is what happened to me last night. Yesterday was Wednesday, our regular Celebrate Recovery night. I was the one scheduled to give my testimony to the group. In my testimony I don't talk about my coming in touch with little me, all this is too time consuming and a testimony isn't to be any longer than 30 minutes. I tell that I had three years of intense counseling and leave it at that. As I got into my share group after giving my testimony I experienced some emotions not yet felt. My share group knows I'm in the process of writing this book. The share group had each of the attendees talking about the impact of tonight's testimony on them and how it could help them with their own personal struggles. This is routine for share group following a testimony. It was now my turn to share. I had just finished writing the part about little Earnie's first comments to me and my response to him from my journal. So, my connection to this was raw last night. I told this to the men in the group but in doing so I almost lost control of myself with convulsive sobs. I did get it together but I was shocked to find that level of intensity within me still. I have always hated the fact that I have this deep emotional level. It somehow connects to my father's intense anger that was used so abusively on all of us boys and girls too at times. I'm learning even in writing this book that I am still growing into the appreciation of my emotions. I am not my father and that fear is only a fear--not a reality. Satan has been hugely diligent in keeping this lie in front of me as though it were true. I say all this because in writing this I sense a huge relief and a sense of letting go of something I've hated. In fact, so many of the men in our group thanked me for being able to allow my emotions to be seen. Well, this has never been a compliment I've wanted to hear until very much of late. I think this must be a step of growth! Now, back to the timeline!

I've already said that little Earnie and I connected daily for several months. Remember that little Earnie was only three or four when our first communications started. I was 59 at the time. We had a lot of catching up to do. Actually, I found I had a lot of healing to experience. The morning of the day Judy used the therapy to help me connect to little Earnie I had written in my journal:

> Jesus, today, walk me through these steps: seeking, shame, fear, anger--these are some of the emotions (protective devices you gave me). As I was "seeking" as a little boy I found others seeking to use me badly. I had a brother who was seeking to use me sexually and a dad who used me for entertainment. If I didn't cooperate with him he'd get angry and I'd get belittled. So, the shame, fear and anger I experienced from dad and his seeking only made the same emotions inside of me harden and hidden--distorted.... Today Jesus, I am beat up. The reality of what was done to me is becoming overwhelming. Now I hear and see in my mind you saying I am to put all this sadness in the "safe place" Judy and I created for the emotions and memories that surfaced

and that I no longer wanted to keep inside of me. My new heart you gave me is a gift. I don't want to harden this new heart with the things that hardened my original one.

This book is taking me back into the journals I've written so I give you the actual writings rather than what I recall of the journal writings. In doing this I'm finding so much I've forgotten. Just two days after I discovered little Earnie he said to me:

Earnie, I trust you. Don't be afraid to trust Jesus and His timing.

I had just written to Jesus before he said this. I was telling Jesus I'd started seeking him and the Holy Spirit when I was in my teens. I wanted them to be my companions, my guides, my protectors. I knew I'd found them and found them with me. I went on to say "I pray the day of full understanding and awareness of you to be soon." It was then that little Earnie said what is written above.

This seems a perfect place to tell about an event two and a half years ago. Kathy and I had gone to Hawaii for our 30 year anniversary. Kathy loves sleeping in and I just don't. So, each morning I'd have a couple hours alone on the deck for devotions and reading ahead of Kathy joining me. This particular morning I had journaled that telling Jesus I hoped it would be time for me to get better acquainted with His Holy Spirit. His response to me was immediate. He said I could never fully get to know the Holy Spirit until I'd gotten better acquainted with my own spirit. This was most troubling since my spirit was what dad had said he needed to kill in me. Yet, today, Jesus said I was to get to know my own spirit better. I've always trusted the voice of God so this became my assignment. The part that follows is more meaningful knowing what I've just written.

The next day little Earnie said:

Jesus, who are you? I am Earnie. I like me. I wish I could like my dad. He's mean to me. Do you love him? Why is he like this? I like my mom. She's sweet to me and everyone. She doesn't like the way dad treats us either.

I was taken back by the questions and statements he was making. I'm sometimes told by others that I'm a confident man in what I do. However, inside myself I don't know confidence. I know sheer determination to do what I do well. Dad had a way of beating confidence out of me thinking it would cause me to have what he called--"a big head". I say this because I was touched by my little self saying "I like me." I have wanted to like me for as long as I've lived. It's gratifying to know there was a time when I was very young that I knew myself and liked myself.

A remarkable thing happened one morning when I was journaling. As I shifted the pen from my left hand to my right one so little Earnie could have voice, he wrote in cursive rather than printing. Being the educator I am I was struck by this. He not only knew how to write cursive, but he was doing it with my right hand. (Boy, does this seem strange telling this, but it is all true!) When I had my next appointment with Judy I shared this event with her. She didn't seem bothered at all. She simply said that little Earnie was growing up and we were getting closer to being one person. Now that felt good!

As "not so little Earnie" and I continued our path of journaling with one another I began to notice that he was often times advising me on matters of the present. I'd journal about things I would be up against and all of a sudden my mind would have a thought from "somewhere" that would be a very good way of dealing with the dilemma. It seemed to be the same voice as my other self, but it seemed much too wise coming from me. I remember going to Judy and telling her this asking if it is possible the voice of Jesus is replacing the voice of the other Earnie? She told me she'd leave that conclusion to Jesus and me. Only we could know this. These years later I will tell you that the two Earnie's have pretty much become one. I now know my little self much better and feel him. There are times like in the share group where I stumble into more emotion unprocessed, but I'm sure that will be the case the rest of my life. The important thing for me is I've actually found an intimate means of communicating with myself as well as with Jesus. I not only can hear Him, but I can respond to Him. Now, I want to add that this isn't some far right Christian fling. I know the Bible well enough to know the deception of Satan's voice. I've lived with his deceptive ways all my life and spent much of my life believing many of the lies he wanted me to never let go of. This voice within is truly one of God and anchored in His Word. Many times what is said is direct scripture or words from a hymn or song. It is always a reminder or an awakening to something I need to know for the present.

During this time of intense counseling I was having my devotions in the early morning and was reading the book of Ruth. If you are familiar with the Celebrate Recovery Bible you will know that each book of the Bible starts with a connection of the book and the characters therein with the overcoming theme of CR ministry. A quote in it reads:

> *Ruth and Naomi were powerless to change their lives. They needed a rescuer who could and would pay the price of redemption. Boaz became that liberator. Christ had done the same for each of us being both able and willing to pay the ultimate price--his life--to buy us back from our broken lives of hurts, hang-ups and habits....*

As I read this, Christ said to me that this is exactly what He was still wanting to do for me. The book of Ruth tells how Boaz, a relative of Naomi became their Kinsman Redeemer. This is the Biblical name for the rescuer. Christ said he wanted to be my kinsman redeemer, my rescuer. I was no longer needing to try and cover any of my past. He had paid the price for all that was done. The guilt and shame were only within my mind and memories. They were not in the new me if I could only accept Christ's redemptive work.

There is one other incident in Judy's counseling I want to specifically put in this book. This session focused on shame. There had been a few of these sessions where we'd planned an extra hour due to the topic. This wasn't one of them, but it should have been. The word shame has always been one that I melt inside from hearing it. If there is a word that describes how I've always felt, it is SHAME. So, Judy's session this particular day was this crisis word. She began her therapy and I would almost immediately break into uncontrollable sobs. We would stop so I could place the feeling, baggage in the "safe container" we'd created for them. However, this time, I was literally paralyzed. I couldn't lift my arms, I could barely whisper. Judy asked me what I was experiencing. She leaned close to me so she could hear what I was trying to say. I told her I couldn't move my body. She asked where I felt the pain and I said it was all over me. At this point she asked me to call for help. I knew she meant asking God, so I did. In a minute or so she asked what was happening and if help arrived? I told her that no one had come but I was use to that, no one had ever come to help with these problems. She immediately told me to not believe this lie. She reminded me of my kids and grandkids and how I knew God had protective angels watching over them and helping them. This same God was mine too. So, don't give up. I whispered OK and kept waiting.

Almost immediately after Judy had said this to me, two helpers came. Don't ask me how I know this, I just do, but the ones who came were Jesus and God. Judy asked if I had help and I said yes. She asked who God had sent and I said it was Him and Jesus. She then told me to let them lift the shame that was weighing me down into the container. They did this for me. At that point they were gone.

When the emotions of this subsided, Judy asked me to let her know what took place. I told her they had done just as she said, lifted the shame into the container never to be weighing me down again to the point of paralysis. She reminded me to be sure and thank them. We had to end this session quickly as we hadn't planned for this to be needing so much additional time. I hurriedly left as her next client was already waiting. I was working with a school that day following this appointment. As I was driving to the school I told Jesus and God, "Thanks for coming today to lift my shame." I also then asked, "Why didn't you send an angel like Judy said?" The answer was instantaneous, "We didn't send an angel because we wanted to come and do this ourselves." With this I almost drove off the highway. I was crying all over again. The belief I had of not being worthy of them just was no longer going to hold water. Here they had come on their own. I know this was to convince me of my worthiness to them. I've always been a firm believer of someone's worthiness to God. I just never had this conviction for me. I'm fully aware of the research which states that our first image of God is primarily set from the image we have of our earthly father. The image of my worthwhileness to dad was anything but worthy. The thankful humility I felt with God and Jesus coming to take away the very SHAME that I thought always kept them at a distance was overwhelming. This is a good example of the lies Satan had wanted me to always believe. God was beginning to shatter this lie for me.

I'm feeling compelled to insert a current item that is occurring regarding the writing of this book. I had finished yesterday's writing with the information about SHAME and God's mighty work for me, of showing up with Jesus to lift the shame from me and then His voice telling me of my value to them. That rocked my boat when it happened and it did again after writing about it yesterday. I know when I feel this way I need to spend time with "the team": God, Jesus and The Holy Spirit during my devotional time to re-anchor myself. Just this morning I finished my Bible reading and began to journal. I asked God what He wanted me to know about yesterday. He simply reminded me that we (He and I) are writing this book together. The voice of the book, even though man may think it is mine, is His. The thoughts from fear I may have during the writing of it come from a past that is dying. The only thing keeping this past alive is my feeding it by acting on the fears rather than seeing them as they are—FEARS, not reality. This ties directly into the worthiness I thought I never had and must earn. To have God remind me of this during my devotions today makes me much more able to move forward with this writing.

As the counseling continued Judy thought I should have Kathy come to a session with me. The following week she came. I don't recall all of the specifics of the session, but it was centering around the topic of "my identity". I was asked to define who I am. I quickly said that I'm a gardener, singer and an educator. I said that because these three things are the very things in life where I've found success. This success has been confirmed by others around me. Judy then said that these were things I do but she was wanting to know who I AM, not what I do. This buffaloed me. I couldn't even begin to think what in the world she was trying to get from me. My assignment for the coming week was to give this thought, talk with Kathy and return ready to give her this information.

The coming week arrived with Kathy and me in Judy's office. When she asked me what I had determined I simply couldn't answer. I had determined nothing. She then asked Kathy to look at me and I was to look at her. She was to tell me who I am to her. She used words like kind and gentle, determined, able to confront, and more. She went on to give many examples of ways describing these characteristics of who I am. Judy asked if I believed them to be true and I said I guess so. As we worked through the session with Judy guiding me into differentiating between actual work we do and characteristics of our person, I could mentally agree with her. In fact, in my mind, it made perfect sense. I could easily differentiate someone else's work from personal characteristics. Towards the end of the session Judy asked me if I were ready to have surgery? We were going to remove the belief that I am a gardener, singer and educator and instead I would be the characteristics described by Kathy that I personally possessed.

During this procedure I could actually visualize the scalpel cutting through this attachment severing it from me. The reality of this, however, was devastating. Judy, following the procedure, said, "Don't you feel more free now?" My response, I think, shocked her. I told her if I had to walk out of her office right now I'd want to walk immediately in front of a semi-truck going 75 mph. She was sending me into the world I'd been hiding from as someone I didn't know from Adam. We talked a little more about this and I agreed to call her if I came up against these difficult moments.

The next morning I was simply overcome with fear. The quartet I sing in was singing for a banquet later that day and I was no longer a singer. What would this great friend of mine think if he were to be singing with someone who isn't a singer? I have been a fake all my life! (This sounds ridiculous as I write it today, but 5 years ago, it was a panic-attack). That morning I drove to Mike's house as I had to confront this with him. He needed to know who I really was now that I wasn't in denial anymore. I called ahead and his wife told me he was out mowing the lawn but by the time I arrived he should be done. I got there just as he was making the final rounds with his mower.

Mike and I went into the house and he asked what was on my mind. I started by saying, "If I were to tell you I'm not a singer, would you still want to sing with me? I wish you could have seen the look on his face! He and I had been singing together by now for 40+ years. He said he didn't think he understood what I was saying. I told him I'd just had a counseling session the afternoon before and I'd found I was not a singer. This wasn't any longer my identity. I had to be something else. I felt like I had been betraying him all these years trying to be something I wasn't. Not only was I doing that to Mike, but I was also doing this to the other two members of our quartet. These words are close to what was said, but I was such an emotional mess that morning, I can't recall the specifics of this. Mike said something like, "Earnie, I'm not sure the point you are trying to make here, but if you think I've sung with you all these years because you were a singer, you are way off base." He then rattled off some things similar to what Kathy had said in the counseling session the previous afternoon. He assured me we were friends who sang together and not singers who did this.

I asked him if he were ok singing with me and his response and facial expression was very telling to me—he had no idea I was so confused! He looked like he wanted to shake me into a reality I should have known long before now. However, Mike himself is a very kind and thoughtful man. He said again that whatever I had thought I was that made him want to sing with me must have been false. He didn't question whether I was a good singer or not, he sang with me because of the person I am. Having this conversation with him helped me see that the same was true for me with him. I sang with Mike because of the person he was and along with that, he was a second tenor. I had thought I would need to have this same conversation with the others in the quartet before that afternoon, but having talked with Mike I was beginning to understand the depth of my mistaken identity.

Having had the talk with Mike, God began to help me address some life-long defects of thinking. Anytime in my growing up years a compliment was made to me, I would immediately get belittled by dad and told I would get the "big-head" if I believed it. My junior year in high school when I won the Oregon state solo contest in the tenor division dad was relentless for a couple weeks belittling me and using that "big-head" talk. He'd say things like "You're just too good for this family, you might as well pack your bags and never come back." I would wonder why he'd say that? I loved everyone in my family and would never not want to see them again.

Words like gentle and kind describing me were labeled sissy and baby or in high school, Hazel. Other words like "able to confront" were said to be "too good for your britches" and "get off your high horse" and accompanied with beatings in younger years. I say all this because "who I am" couldn't be all the things I was. These were the very elements of Earnie that I thought had made him a failure to his dad. Now, God wanted me to recognize who was wrong. I wasn't the mistake, the error after all. God had intentionally made me this way. In fact, Judy pointed out if I hadn't had these characteristics so deeply embedded in me I would likely not be in the place I'm in today—successful in life. She told me that most men with this background are either in prison or had a prison record. Even though I hadn't recognized these characteristics as ME, God was having me use them to keep me successful in life.

I must confess that I battle with this mental image routinely today. I still have the strong impulses to flee when I'm done singing, or done with any major work so I won't hear any comments. I don't want to have a good feeling that I did well so I won't hear the voice of dad shouting in my ear/mind. I do, however, make myself remain present after events hoping no one recognizes the deep impulses I feel. Mrs. Denman, my high school music teacher, used to tell me to discipline myself to remain in the room where we'd sung. In my high school years I'd exit the minute the program finished. She said it was the polite and proper thing to do. Some members of an audience will want to talk with the singer/s and I should not rob them of that opportunity. I had always wanted to tell her, "BUT....", but, I never could. When I finally sent her my testimony for Celebrate Recovery so she knew my background and could connect these oddities to my past, we talked on the phone for a couple hours. She said she had no idea just how tough life was for me. I assured her in spite of how tough it was, she was my "human savior" God was using to keep me afloat.

CHAPTER 20

Mom

This chapter is almost one within a chapter. All I am going to write in it will be part of the three years of counseling, but Mom needs a chapter unto herself. Mom was every single one of her kids' HERO. If I were to try and describe why HERO fits for her, it would be a little difficult to put into words, but I'm going to take a stab at it. The first thing that comes to mind is that mom stayed with dad for 73 years of marriage. Why she did that is something almost no other person on earth would have done. Mom's patience was endless as well as her tolerance. She was much like her own father, my grandpa Wretling. They were quiet people, very introverted and yet friendly. Mom was faithful, steady, punctual and consistent to the end. She never talked about these traits, but she modeled them every moment of every day. If I embody any of them in my own walk it is due to mom's modeling.

Before I go any further I want to tell one little story about my grandpa Wretling. My grandpa and grandma Wretling would come to our farm every year in the summer while we were on the farm at Adrian, OR. The summer I graduated from high school they made their annual trip. On a Sunday afternoon that summer grandpa took me aside, pulled out his wallet and gave me two one dollar bills. He said it was my graduation present. I had never remembered getting a present from either of them but he gave me the money and then said, be sure to use it to buy something special. That two dollars stayed in my own billfold for months before I could finally decide what was special enough to warrant grandpa Wretling's money. I was well into my freshman year in college before it hit me what to buy. I went to the music store and bought a copy of the music for "The Lord's Prayer". In those days I sang this song quite often for weddings and church events. To think grandpa's money was used for this was perfect. The cost of the sheet music was $1.98. So, there I had it!

To think I was needing counseling about mom just didn't seem right to me. She had been my anchor, not my hindrance. However, each time I'd had counseling it had been brought to my attention—I must work through some elements with mom. Finally getting as far along as I was with the counseling I was now willing to address anything if it would help unravel the many years of torment. Questions were asked like, "Where was your mom when your dad was beating you?" "Did your mom know about Rich's abuse?" "What did your mom say to you about the abuse?" "What did your mom say after a beating from your father?" It didn't matter what the question was, my response to them was, "I don't know" or "Nothing." Mom never entered into the beatings from dad or never addressed with me the sexual abuse of Rich. The time I told dad when I was around 11 years old, mom also knew.

Once I began to think through the fact that mom never came to "little Earnie's" side to ask how he was or to question what was going on with Rich, I began to understand why I should work this through in order to have a healthier self-image. In one of the therapy sessions I recalled the only time I remember my mom touching me intimately. I was about five or six when I had fallen out of the pecan tree in our yard in Escondido. It was a Sunday afternoon and three or four of us kids were in the tree climbing around. I remember falling out and the next thing I recall is being on the couch in the living room with my head in mom's lap and she was stroking my back. I suppose I must have been knocked out for a few minutes. When I came to I just laid there thinking this was nice. I have no other memory of mom's physical touch. I've not thought this was negligence as I am not a physical touch person anyway. Kathy would be the first to tell you I don't receive touch well nor do I offer it. It has been said this is likely due to the physical abuse and sexual abuse in my past. I know there's some truth to this, but in reality I think I'm put together much like mom in this. Don't misunderstand this—I do like a healthy hug. What I can't receive is a surprise hug or a spontaneous hug that I'm not anticipating. These unexpected times of touch quickly take me to the brink. I want to get better about this, but it hasn't happened yet.

I've always wanted to ask mom why she didn't ask about Rich or ask about how we were in regards to a beating from dad. I've surmised why she didn't, but I'd love to know straight from her. I'll save these questions for a heavenly conversation. In the counseling sessions I can honestly say I discovered a false belief that no one cared how I was. I needed to protect myself as best I could and wall off from my feelings all that I could of the abuse from either Rich or dad.

There was one time early in my sophomore year of college when I was elected president of our college Sunday School class. It wasn't a big deal because all it meant was welcoming newcomers to the class, working with the teacher for parties, and leading in prayer at times. However, I felt good about it and called to tell mom and dad. Dad told me I needed to resign from it. It would keep me from coming home on weekends. I said that wouldn't be the case. I'd just go back on Saturday nights rather than after church on Sundays. Nonetheless, he said he wanted me to resign. I thought and stewed about this. It was the first time I hadn't done such a thing as resign when dad gave the order. I was now in college and I knew he was wrong about his thinking. I wrote mom and dad a letter to tell them I was going to keep the position and they didn't need to worry. I'd be coming home as often as I had my freshman year.

The following weekend I did go home. It was fall and potato harvest time. I arrived very early Saturday morning knowing everyone would be headed to the potato field at sunlight. As I arrived, dad was warming up the tractor and so I jumped onto the back end of it to ride with him to the field. Grandma and Grandpa Wretling were there at the time. When I got on the tractor dad began to push me off saying, "Get out of here, go back to that college and stay there. You don't belong here anymore. All you want to do is your own thing over there anyway. You're too good for us you think so get out of here." He pushed hard enough that I fell back. I got up off the ground and ran off onto the hills on the backside of our place. I did some crying and yelling to get this off my chest and came back to the house. Mom was outside hanging clothes on the line. I went up to her and yelled, "Tell me what I did was wrong, tell me!" This was the only time mom ever addressed something like this with me. She looked at me and said, "No Earnie, you weren't wrong." All the other scores of times I'd asked her similar questions she'd say, "You need to do what your father says." I told her thanks. She said to go on out to the field. Dad would get over it. I spent the day in the field with my grandpa. He and I threw potatoes left by the digger into the trucks.

Two weeks after this event I came home again. You would think this chaos had never happened. Dad was friendly all weekend. I went back on Saturday evening and he had no problem with it. We never had another conversation about any of this.

I'm sure mom had thoughts about dad and Rich's abusive ways. Mom wasn't one to confront conflict. She was a peacemaker at all costs. I think the cost of what all the abuse had done was just going to have to be paid some other way than having mom confront any of it. I truly understand this. But in spite of any cost, I had to confront the consequences on me from the absence of mom. Somehow, I believe, this absence of mom also had its own impact on me believing how much God valued me. The silence of mom fed into what I thought was a silence of God. This led me to believe neither cared that much for me.

The conversations I'd love to have had with mom never took place. Mom died in 1999 from a massive heart attack and stroke which took place within seconds from one another. They left mom completely paralyzed. Her throat was paralyzed so she couldn't swallow taking in liquid or food. She made slight facial expressions and could blink her eyes. Her heart only had about 25% usage also. She lived 8 days. These were grueling days too. The doctor gave us the consequences of giving mom life support or letting nature do its final work. All of us kids met the evening of the doctor's visit and knew we had to let her go. The next day I did my best to convey the message to her. I told her she had spent her life reflecting Jesus to each and everyone of us kids. Now we were going to let her go into His arms. My youngest sister, Polly and I were able to be with her when she passed into heaven. Dear Polly was able to sing hymns to mom during this last evening. I was too upset seeing and watching her body give up life to join Polly in the hymns. This was one time when I had no strength to give except my presence.

The first counselor I had said it was much easier to confront counseling needs in life and I've talked about doing this with dad. The advice to do this hadn't been given ahead of mom dying. Thank goodness what I needed to confront after death was with mom and not with dad. God knew I needed the time with dad while he was still living. It was about 6 weeks after mom had died that I had an actual conversation with her. There is a little more I need to tell ahead of this however.

The afternoon before mom's stroke and heart attack, several of us kids met with mom and the social worker of Caldwell Hospital. Dad had been in the hospital for almost two weeks. We had been called in three times during this period to say our good-byes to dad. Each time he rallied. This afternoon we were talking to the social worker because the next day they were releasing dad. They needed to know if they should release him to come home or to a rehab center. Mom was pretty insistent that she could in no way handle dad if he were to come home. We assured her that we boys would take turns spending the nights with her so she'd never be on her own. We also assured her that our sisters and wives would trade off the daytime hours so she wouldn't be alone then, either. We all agreed to this but one could easily read mom's extreme stress level. That very night was the stroke and heart attack. Each one of us kids struggled with being responsible for mom dying when she did. She was the very person we wanted to have living with us after dad died. Now she was gone and we were left with decisions about dad. The odd thing about all this is that the day dad was to be released he took another turn for the worse and was in the hospital the eight days before mom died. The day of mom's funeral turned out to be the day we admitted dad to a nursing home. He never came home again. He was in three different ones over the next three and a half years before his death.

Now, having this understanding, I can proceed with my devotional time six weeks after mom died. I started with a journaling conversation that morning telling Jesus how badly I felt about mom dying because we wouldn't let dad go somewhere besides home. He assured me He was responsible for mom's timing, not me or any other of us kids. It was then that I wrote I just didn't know who would model Jesus for us now that she was gone. Instantly I saw my mom standing before me holding my two hands in hers. She said in her sweet, little voice, "Earnie, I want you to follow the same Jesus I've always followed." Hearing that message meant the world to me. Those words coming from mom somehow gave life to her again. Her human body was dead, but not mom. I truly needed to know this little lady we all loved and adored was still with us in spirit. I would be spending eternity with her, too.

When mom died, we buried her on Sept. 1 and had a celebration service following the burial. We had a beautiful pink rose floral arrangement made for her. After the burial it lay on top of the grave. Following the celebration service for mom three of us boys took dad to the Homedale nursing home. I finally got home around 5:30-6:00 pm. Upon walking in the house I realized I'd not taken any roses from the arrangement on mom's grave for my two California sisters. They had been here during mom's hospital stay but had gone back to California after her death. One needed to return to work and so they were unable to be here for the funeral. I told them I'd save a rose for each of them. The day had been rather warm for early September. I knew the roses would be wilted but I would do the best I could. I got in my car and quickly drove again to the grave site. Approaching the grave I saw scores of wilted pink roses. I was about to cry again as I got to the head of the grave. There, looking right at me, were two long stem pink roses standing very erect. I knew one was for Bonnie and one was for Alice. I took them, thanked God for His kind thoughtfulness and went home. Bonnie and Alice still have these two dried roses.

I've grown into some critical understandings about mom. First and foremost, she was faithful to the end. Her greatest gift to me and to each of us kids was that she stayed. No matter how awful the situations were, she stayed. In addition to staying, she always participated with us. She worked alongside of us in the fields hoeing beets and anything else she could do. She mothered 12 kids experiencing the death of one early on and the death of another in his prime years. She also endured institutionalizing one. In all of this, she stayed. I give great tribute to mom for this. She didn't talk to me about some critical things I'd wanted to talk about, but I'm now fine waiting until she and I can hop over to Saturn, getting away from the crowd, and talking to our hearts' content!

A year after my father had died my wife Kathy and I were taking a summer trip to Southern California to visit Alice and Bonnie. Mom and Dad's home hadn't had anyone go through it to distribute what little there was to the children or grandkids. I knew mom had a place setting of china for six. I wanted to get that and take it to my sis Bonnie. I also wanted to see what else might be there I could have as a token of them. My brother Ralph was the executor for them so I called and had him meet me at their home. I walked in the house and immediately had to step back outside. My breath was gone. On the kitchen table was a box of 50 pint jars of canned green beans I had placed there a year before. The morning following my taking them to mom and dad, dad had gone to the hospital. He and mom had never returned to their home from that time. After I pulled myself together I re-entered with Ralph. I found the place settings and looked around a little more. I discovered quilts mom and my sister-in-law Jann had made. I found the children's Bible mom had read to us kids when we were very young. I found an album my brother Don had made and given to mom and dad. It was fun to give these keepsakes to their new recipients. I kept the children's Bible. About five years ago my own grandson was spending a night with grandma and me. The next morning when I was having my devotions he came in to the den where I was and asked what I was doing. I said I was reading about Jesus. He wanted me to read to him about Jesus. I found the children's Bible mom use to read to us. I told him this was very old and I'd read a story out of it my mom use to read to me. I chose the one where Jesus was telling his followers to gather the children to come around him for he loved them and their friend he'd always be. At the end of the story it said that one could ask Jesus into their heart if they wanted. My grandson said he wanted to do this and would I help him. It was a precious moment to pray with my grandson as he asked Jesus to come into his heart. And, it was from the children's Bible storybook I had read to me by mom.

The Three Years Conclude

As Judy and I worked through the stages of recovery each week I was becoming more and more awake to all that I had buried. I mentioned I had a safe place where I'd put all the emotional baggage that came out of the sessions. I had no idea this container was so HUGE. It just kept taking it and keeping it locked tight. My body isn't that big, but my emotional baggage capacity had been much larger than I'd ever wanted it to be.

By the end of the second year of counseling I knew it was time to take my journey to my sister Bonnie. Kathy and I had arranged to take a week to go to Southern California visiting both Bonnie and Alice. By now they lived in the same subdivision. This made it wonderful for visiting them. I could walk to both their homes within minutes. Bonnie still works so I'd asked if she'd take a day off just for the two of us. I was wanting to go through my Celebrate Recovery testimony with her. Alice had heard it by now, but it was more significant for me to tell Bonnie since she was at home during all my years of abuse from Rich. She just didn't have a clue about them.

On the drive to S. California Kathy and I stayed the night in Hawthorne, Nevada. It was early the next morning and we were about 10 miles out of the town and well into the high desert country. I started to ask Kathy why she loved me. She said she just did. That just wasn't enough. I wanted to know WHY she loved me? What was loveable about me? I had focused so long on the damage of me and its effects on me that that's all I could see of me. There was nothing redeeming about me. Why would she love me except out of sheer selflessness. She began to tell me the complimentary aspects of my personality--both of them! (That's a joke!) There were four I believe. I don't mean to be trite about this. It's just hard to write about positive characteristics when they are suppose to represent me. Kathy assured me she didn't love me because she felt sorry for me. I became so overwhelmed with emotion I had to stop for a moment to get my composure so I could drive again. I suppose I could have let Kathy drive but I needed the driving to keep me focused on something beyond the visit with Bonnie.

The day Bonnie and I had together was one I'll forever treasure. She chose a nice park-like setting by a lake. It was mid-week so no one was near us making it safe for all the conversation we needed. What took about 25 minutes to read in a Celebrate Recovery setting took four hours with us. Of course Bonnie knew much of the past--she was right there. The part of Rich was to take her totally by surprise and the damage from it was even greater. The two of us have been close all our lives. She said she felt like she'd somehow abandoned me when I needed her most. Of course I'd never felt that way. The reason I was wanting to read this to her now was so she, the sis I had always been so close to, would know the SECRET I'd always kept from everyone. I had told Alice because it was easier to tell her. She wasn't at home during all this time. Alice is 16 years older than I so she was gone by the time all of it took place. Alice is very compassionate and I love her as my sis. It was just that Bonnie and I were close during all this time and now I wanted nothing unknown between us. We went to lunch and spent the rest of the day enjoying the time we had together.

As the counseling was moving from therapy to just counseling Judy and I began working to see if I was ready to move forward on my own. Sessions would happen with a little therapy to see if there were any blockages we'd encounter. We eventually got to the place where Judy told me she thought I was ready to step out on my own.

About this same time I was wrapping up a three year period of working with some schools in the neighboring town of Nampa, Idaho. The school district that fall had discovered some debt that was significant enough that the superintendent and assistant superintendent resigned as well as several others in the district office. An interim superintendent had been hired to assist unraveling all this entanglement. On my own, I'd begun to think seriously about writing this book. I thought that now would be a good time to put on paper what God had done for me in hopes others would find the strength to confront their own secrets, walls, and bondage. I had contacted a book publishing company and was talking through a contract with them.

It was the week before Christmas and I was closing the day with a school in Nampa having a meeting with their leadership team. About 30 minutes before the meeting ended my cell phone went off and I quickly silenced it. After the meeting

I noted the call had come from some place in the district. Showing the number to the principal she said it was the district office. I called it back to find they were trying to reach me to talk about my interviewing the next day with them. They needed someone to unravel the federal program dollars that had been frozen by the State Department of Education due to some misuse. I found out later that it was the State that suggested they call me. I went in the next day to meet with the interim superintendent, publicist, human resource officer, acting assistant superintendent and chief financial officer. We talked about what the job would look like and agreed we would talk the next day giving both parties a chance to "sleep on this", (for me it was to pray about it). The following afternoon I was on the phone with the publishing company when the district called offering me the work. I then accepted it along with closing the book contract.

Within a week after starting the new work I knew I would need to be resigning all the other consulting work I was doing. I had been doing what's called capacity building in a couple other schools as well as working with a state level professional project called Idaho Leads. These projects had others to do the work, this new responsibility was needing my full attention.

About a month into this work I had the previous year's money unfrozen. I was now needing to get the current year's money freed. By mid-March this was done and approved. It was at this time that Jesus showed me in my devotional time He was using the work I was doing in Nampa to parallel the work He was doing to unravel all the messes in my life and the defects of my thinking.

I've been with the district now for two years and presently working with the last six months when I will be finished. The district has new leadership and is building a strong common purpose with vision and defined steps. This is exactly what God has been doing for me these past couple years. The practices that had me frozen in place were being redone with purpose and meaning. The wrong thinking is being corrected and I've joined God's team giving Him full charge of me. So now the timing was ripe for the book's writing.

Finding Freedom

Have you ever thought a haircut could bring a sense of peace? As I've been working through the writing of this chapter I was recently awakened to the sense of peace a haircut brings. One of our men in Celebrate Recovery recently gave his testimony. He mentioned that he'd never had a barber haircut growing up. Hearing this I had this jolt of disgust run through my system remembering back to the awful experiences of dad's haircuts. One thing about me, I love the work I do and I love being involved in the work I enjoy. I like to look nice, but once I'm dressed I have no more thoughts of appearance. I think about work. So, what does this have to do with a haircut? Let me explain. All through my growing up years my dad cut my hair. This wasn't just true for me, but he did this with all of us boys. I thought little about it as a young child. I didn't know a haircut was important except to keep it out of your face and things like that. What I did notice about a haircut was that I never wanted dad to cut it when he was in one of his nasty moods. All of us knew the scars of haircuts: nicked ears from scissors and the embarrassment of a "butch cut" when one wanted hair to have a little length to it. I had never had a professional cut until I went to college. I didn't even know what to do when I went in the barbershop. My roommate told me there would be chairs typically to sit in and do that. The barber would tell me when he was ready for me. When this actually took place, I recall the barber asking me what I wanted my haircut to look like? All I could think was, "Not like dad's." I finally said something like, "Could you take the way I have it combed and just make it be smooth looking so it doesn't have the appearance of a butcher?" I then told him this was my first barber cut. He chuckled and cut my hair nicely. What is amazing is that once I experienced this barber cut, I never gave any thought to my hair. I could relax and think only about what I was doing. My youngest daughter is a licensed beautician and she now cuts my hair. I chuckle thinking about my early years of haircuts and how ugly I felt afterwards growing up and how self-conscious this left me. Now, I'm at peace and a little part of that peace is a good haircut.

When Alice's husband, Tom, passed away from liver cancer a few years ago, she wanted me to conduct his service. I would have never thought I would be asked to do something like this because I wouldn't have been worthy of such an important thing. However, Alice and family didn't think that. These kind of thoughts I was learning were about my own thinking of me. I needed a "heart of flesh" about who I am. God was remaking me to see myself as valuable to others. Tom's service was a blessed time and a wonderful tribute to him--a great man. I loved the opportunity to do this for Alice and her family.

A year or so after Tom's service, Bonnie's younger son was getting married. They wanted me to do their ceremony. Much like with Tom's service, I felt so unworthy. This time however, I didn't contest it, I thanked them for the opportunity. I paid to get an "on-line" certificate legitimizing me to conduct the service, but being a wise nephew, he and his bride got married by the justice of the peace and I conducted what we called "the spiritual ceremony". That made it all much easier! While we were in California for the wedding ceremony, Bonnie's husband, Randy, asked me if I'd baptize him. This is what brought me to tears. I was the most unworthy of all people to conduct such a sacred moment. Yet, I wanted to tell my brother-in-law no because I was operating from my past instead of from my freed body. We did it and it was such a special time. God keeps chipping away at this belief system (character defects as Celebrate Recovery says).

Just this last summer of 2014, I was asked by a couple in our Celebrate Recovery group to conduct a marriage renewal for them as they were having their 25th wedding anniversary. The man had been one who had become a Christian resulting from the time in Celebrate Recovery. Their marriage had totally turned around from this. They wanted me to do this honor for them. I was so humbled. He told me I was like the father figure he never had. How could this man find a father figure in someone who kept his past hidden because of his awful identity? Why would someone say this about me when they knew my past? Once again, God keeps chipping away at my belief system. God keeps teaching me that the past Satan wants me to believe is my identity, is simply a past. It is not a good one by any means, but it is what happened to me. It is not what was created in me. The heart, the soul, the mind, the body are all what God created. Satan has truly wanted me to remain paralyzed by this past, but God wants me free from it so I can use the mess of it to be a message for someone else's freedom as He is providing my own.

Our quartet sings for some of the assisted living homes in our valley. It is always a blessed time to do this. A few years ago, Mike, who puts our order together when we sing, wanted me to give my testimony to the group of elderly people. I told him I thought it was completely out of line. These were folks who needed to be lifted up in song, not laden with the burden of my ugly past. He said to trust his judgment as God had wanted him to have me do this. I consented and told a 5 minute summary of my past and God's work to redeem it. What I was not expecting at all was how many of the attendees wanted to talk when we were done. Two different ones held my hand saying they had been abused all their childhood years and had never told anyone. Even their deceased husbands had never known. They were so relieved to hear me tell mine so they could finally say out loud what they'd kept as their tarnished secret. I've said earlier that in Celebrate Recovery, we have the statement that God takes our mess and makes it a message. That is exactly what he is doing with mine and I will be forever grateful.

It is one thing to give my testimony to a group of folks in Celebrate Recovery, it is another thing to do it for a group of people I've always thought were better than me. These would be the folks in church on a Sunday morning or those in an assisted living place. These folks don't need to be troubled with someone's story. I would hear the voice of dad in my head saying things like, "Quit feeling sorry for yourself," "You don't need to try and get attention for yourself," "You're just telling this to put me down. Well, I hope you are proud of yourself!" I fight these voices knowing now they are the voices of Satan.

They aren't even dad's voice. I know beyond a shadow of a doubt that dad is proud of me. I say this very humbly.

Another item I've found in finding freedom is the singing with the men in our quartet. I've talked already about how disappointed I knew they'd be when I found in my identity that I'm not a singer. I talked about going to see Mike and what he said to me. In the last few years I've never heard from any of them about their disappointment. In fact, they say complimentary things—things I'd never expect to hear from them. It is amazing to me how much God is wanting me to learn. Each one of our singing engagements is an opportunity to help someone find a step to freedom that someone may not find otherwise. I've yet to tell my story when I didn't hear from at least one person who said—"Thank you so much, this is my story, too."

I've mentioned the Serenity Prayer earlier and the line in it that says: "Taking one day at a time, one moment at a time, accepting hardship as a pathway to peace." This applies to finding freedom, too. Now that I'm more fully awake to my past being a past and not an identity, I have to use this line as a promise from God. No matter what God is placing before me in the day, I only need to take the day, the moment I'm presently in and do what is expected. The person God made me to be is sufficient for it. God is showing me that His Holy Spirit will speak to mine giving guidance, wisdom, and direction. My role is to listen and respond. As I do this I find the pathway to peace. God never fails. He never intended for me to be the "error" as in the title of this book. He created me to be an "heir" of Christ's redeeming love on the Cross. My belief system had to be transformed and that is exactly what God and His team: Jesus and The Holy Spirit have been doing. That is why the path I've been taking, reflected in the book cover, leads only to the Cross--the starting place and the ending place for each day and each moment of the day. The result of this--"a pathway to peace".

CONCLUSION

Matthew 11:29 says, "Take my yoke upon you and learn of me, for I am meek and lowly of heart and ye shall find rest for your soul." (King James Bible)

Being a farm boy and a gardener at heart, I have learned much about working animals that helped with the farming. The idea of taking a yoke upon you never seemed "comforting". However, about three years ago I was compelled by this verse to make it real for me. Each morning at the end of my devotions I would lift my arms fully into the air asking God to place his yoke upon me. For several months I kept this up, feeling really uncomfortable with the thought of it but doing it out of sheer discipline for God had told me to. What became incredible was the ease of having this yoke placed upon me. The yoke became a tool, a focus for which God would actually restrain me when I was needing it. Sometimes it would be with words, sometimes it would be to speak up with words given to me. Sometimes, it would be to place a hand on someone's shoulder and say nothing.

The yoke of man is a discipline of labor. The yoke of God is a gift of grace. I have lived under the yoke of man and the yoke of dad's voice much of my life. Taking the yoke of God and learning how comforting and focusing it is helps me to know why the last of the verse says, "and ye shall find rest for your soul". I've longed for rest, for peace of mind and worked so hard for it. Yet, work doesn't get me there. It is surrender that does. Lifting my arms to God, taking on the yoke knowing that I am "meek and lowly of heart". That is when I find the "rest for my soul". Rest is exactly what it is. That rest is the freedom I've always sought. It can be yours too. Don't quit until the miracle happens!

Lastly, I'm learning there is a hunger that comes with freedom. The freedom that Christ offers us is free. However, there is a compelling desire once the freedom is found to not keep it to yourself. Thus, the reason for taking the risk to write this book, to lay oneself bare to the world so others can see and know they are not alone. The isolation of secrets, the shame and fear from abuse doesn't need to keep us in the prison where one may presently reside. I pray that you, the reader, if there is a prison surrounding you, will take the necessary risk to seek the help. It is likely much closer than you would think and it is likely much safer than you could ever dream. God bless you.

RESOURCES

CELEBRATE RECOVERY
celebraterecovery.com

Judy Hudson, Counselor
Hudson Counseling
1909 S. 10th
Caldwell, Idaho 83607
(208) 228-0301

Earnie Lewis, author
earniele@msn.com

CPSIA information can be obtained
at www.ICGtesting.com
Printed in the USA
FSOW02n1012020915
10608FS